The Battle for the Swiepwald

Austria's fatal blunder at Königgrätz, the climactic battle of the Austro-Prussian War 3 July 1866

Oberst Ernst Heidrich

Edited by Gerard W. Henry

Translated by Frederick P. Steinhardt

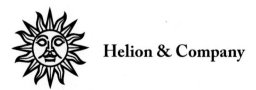 Helion & Company

Helion & Company Limited
Unit 8 Amherst Business Centre
Budbrooke Road
Warwick
CV34 5WE
England
Tel. 01926 499 619
Email: info@helion.co.uk
Website: www.helion.co.uk
Twitter: @helionbooks
Visit our blog http://blog.helion.co.uk/

Published by Helion & Company 2022
Designed and typeset by Mach 3 Solutions Ltd (www.mach3solutions.co.uk)
Cover designed by Paul Hewitt, Battlefield Design (www.battlefield-design.co.uk)

English translation © Gerard W. Henry 2022
Illustrations open source
Maps drawn by George Anderson © Helion & Company 2022

ISBN 978-1-915070-49-4

British Library Cataloguing-in-Publication Data.
A catalogue record for this book is available from the British Library.

For details of other military history titles published by Helion & Company Limited contact the above address, or visit our website: http://www.helion.co.uk.

We always welcome receiving book proposals from prospective authors.

Contents

Pharm. Mag.

Ernst Heidrich

k. u. k. Militär-Medicamenten-Verwalter

This translation is dedicated with affection and respect to the memory of the late Professor Richard Holmes CBE TD JP, in acknowledgement of his patience, courtesy and encouragement over many years.

G.W. Henry

List Of Illustrations

List of Maps

Editor's Foreword to the English Edition

Colonel (*Oberst*) Ernst Heidrich was a serving officer in the KuK (Kaiserlich und Königlich, Imperial and Royal) Army when he wrote this exceptionally detailed monograph *Der Kampf Um Den Svibwald Am 3. Juli 1866* [*The Battle for the Swiepwald of 3rd July 1866*], which was published by Sadowa Press in 1902.

Particulars of his early life are sparse, but we know he was born in the town of Horschitz (Horice) and attended the high school in Hradec Kralove (Königgrätz) before being commissioned into the Austro-Hungarian Army. He seems to have served principally as an administrative officer, first as pharmacy superintendent in the fortress hospital at Josefov between 1880 and 1900, and later in the same capacity at Sarajevo (Bosnia). In the decennial Imperial census of 1900, Heidrich recorded his nationality as Czech not German, possibly to the detriment of his military career. He was living in Prague in 1918 when the Empire finally collapsed and he died there in 1922. His son, Arnošt (Ernst) Heidrich, was a noted Czech diplomat, a delegate to the League of Nations and a leading figure in the Czech resistance movement during the Second World War when he was imprisoned in Theresienstadt. Following the communist putsch of 1948, he fled with his family to the United States.

The battle of Königgrätz was the largest ever fought in Western Europe until the advent of the First World War and the political consequences were no less epic: the demise of Austria as a European Great Power, the loss of her historic pre-eminence among the German nations, and the final incontestable rise of Prussia. Whether Austria could have prevailed on 3 July 1866 and salvaged her Great Power status is debatable; what is not in question is the part the struggle for the Swiepwald played in her ultimate defeat. Heidrich's definitive account of this 'battle within a battle' takes us through the fighting, hour by hour and foot by bloody foot, in a narrative unsurpassed for detail or accuracy.

This was the first of Ted Steinhardt's translations that I had the privilege to commission and edit (the other being Volume 2 of Theodore Fontane's *Der Deutsche Krieg Von 1866*). As with Fontane, Ted's exceptional knowledge of the period and minute attention to detail is particularly evident in the provision of extensive footnotes. These furnish the reader with an abundance of background material indispensable to a fuller understanding of the text and indeed the war. My job as editor was to render this meticulous translation into a form more readily assimilated by the modern reader. It is not and was never intended to be a word-for-word transliteration.

In 1866 most Prussian line infantry regiments comprised three battalions: the 1st and 2nd *Musketeer* Battalions and the 3rd or *Fusilier* Battalion. Each of the three battalions had four companies and thus each regiment had 12 companies, numbered sequentially 1 to 12 (the last four being *Fusiliers*). Austrian infantry regiments comprised four battalions – three service battalions and one independent fourth battalion – although generally only the three service battalions took to the field. Each Austrian battalion had six companies, and thus each regiment had 18 companies, numbered sequentially 1 to 18. The Austrians frequently paired two companies into a tactical formation known as a 'division', numbered sequentially 1 to 9. To distinguish between an Austrian two-company division, and the larger formation also called a Division but comprising multiple brigades, the two-company Austrian division will be spelled with lower case 'd' while the larger Division with upper case 'D'. In the text, Austrian infantry regiments are designated by their number, and at least once by the name of their Honorary Colonel or *Inhaber* (for example, IR (Infantry Regiment) 12 Archduke William). To avoid lengthy repetition, I have employed my own shorthand. Thus the 2nd Company of the 1st Battalion of the Prussian 66th Infantry Regiment, becomes the 2nd Company Pr. I/66 (the first and second Musketeer battalions are designated I and II, the 3rd or Fusilier Battalion is designated 'F'). Similarly, the 14th Company, 3rd Battalion of the Austrian 4th Infantry Regiment, Hoch und Deutschmeister, becomes 14th Company IR III/4. To avoid confusion, Prussian light infantry units are generally referred to as *Jägers* while Austrian light infantry units are referred to as *Feldjägers*. The chapter entitled 'Configuration of the Swiepwald on 3 July 1866' has been largely re-written and includes several important features which the author omitted to letter. Everything after O (that is, P, Q, R, S, T, W and X) has been added subsequently to make map navigation simpler. Those areas where the timber has been logged (O, N and X) are described as 'cleared'. The author has included three excellent maps of the forest with his original work, however they are really just snapshots. These are included in reduced form in the book but can be downloaded and enlarged from the Helion website. The first map was drawn without troops to acquaint the reader with the topography of the Swiepwald, the second at 10.15 am covers the attack of Brigade Poeckh, and the third at 11.30 am shows the attacks of Brigades Wurttemberg and Saffran. Strobl's series of six maps (Skizze 13–18; see the Bibliography) are more sequenced but do not always fit with Heidrich's narrative. One possible way for the reader to follow this complicated battle is to download the enlarged map and follow the action using counters, or if the reader is in possession of a map case or laminating facilities, mark it up with chinagraph pencils or the equivalent.

The concluding pages of Heidrich's book are devoted to an extraordinarily detailed study of the organisation of the Austrian and Prussian armies. The text is accompanied by numerous charts and tables that can also be accessed through the Helion website.

Finally, I should like to acknowledge two debts. Firstly to my friends Major General John 'DZ' Drewienkiewicz CB CMG and Mr. Andrew Brentnall, with whom I have spent many contented – and contentious hours tramping through the Swiepwald and without whose sharp eyes I should never have discovered Heidrich in the first place. Secondly, to Mrs. Lizzie Holmes for her kind permission to dedicate this volume in memory of her late husband, Professor Richard Holmes.

Gerard W. Henry, January 2022

Translator's Preface to the English Edition

Heidrich's study of the Battle for the Swiepwald is outstanding for its accuracy and detail and is one of the finest action studies I have ever read. After many years of translating and editing German military histories of the First and Second World Wars it has been an exciting adventure to move into the period of the *hyphenated wars* (the Schleswig-Holstein War, the Austro-Prussian War and the Franco-Prussian War), and I decided early on that the best way to avoid errors was to read and study my way into the material I was working on until I knew it thoroughly. That of course, has been the real reward for me – becoming thoroughly immersed in my work as part of a lifetime love affair with history.

I have observed certain conventions throughout this translation. Prussian Corps are in Roman numerals, Prussian armies, Divisions, brigades, regiments, battalions, companies and platoons are generally in Arabic (but see the Editor's Foreword on shortened unit designations). All Austrian formations are in Arabic, however Austrian brigades are identified with the name of the Brigade Commander, e.g. Brigade Saffran.

Ranks and titles such as Archduke (*Erzherzog*), Major General (*Generalmajor*) and Prince (*Prinz*) are generally translated unless there is no suitable English equivalent as with *Feldzeugmeister* or where the distinction between the two would be lost in translation as with *Freiherr* and *Baron*.

Any text which is enclosed by square brackets [ ] has been added by the translator or the editor for edification. Text in curved brackets ( ) has usually been added by the author. Occasionally, for the purpose of clarity, the editor has placed curved brackets around dependent or subordinate clauses.

The spelling of place names is a problem. The original place names are Czech or German, and each author seems to use a different rendition or modification thereof. I have generally used the spelling employed in the work at hand, since that is the spelling used on that source's maps. Major place names, such as Bohemia, Moravia and Saxony, are given as their English equivalents. In the chapter entitled 'Configuration of the Swiepwald on 3 July 1866', the editor has added '[and environs]' naming and lettering a number of features that appear in the narrative but have not been separately identified on the map by the author.

Except for the German *Schritt*, or pace (a German *Schritt* measures approximately 30 inches or 75cms), the author uses metric measurements.

A glance at the Bibliography will provide the reader with the material that I have used and found valuable in understanding Heidrich's study (although it was tempting to extend the Bibliography to include more). It includes basic works on the weaponry, equipment, tactics and technology of the period; histories of the Prussian and Austrian armies; histories of Prussia and the Habsburg Empire; and the specific military history of the Austro-Prussian War.

Frederick P. Steinhardt, Ouray, Colorado, USA, January 2020

The Battle

for the Swiepwald

3rd July,1866.

Compiled from the Austrian and Prussian General Staff studies, as well as the histories of all of the Austrian and Prussian infantry forces that took part in this battle, as well as that of the Austrian 4th Field Artillery Regiment

by

Ernst Heidrich

The profits will be dedicated to the purposes of the Society for the Preservation of the Memorials on the Battle Field of Königgrätz.

Sadova, 1902.

Respectfully dedicated to

His Serene Highness

k. u. k. General der Cavallerie,

Wilhelm *Prinz zu* Schaumburg – Lippe,

as the High Patron

of the

Central Society

for the Preservation

of the Military Memorials from the Year 1866

in Bohemia

by

Ernst Heidrich.

The Horenoves pheasantry

↕

The road from Sendrazic to Horenoves

The historic linden trees with the equine exercise area (manège) to the right. Hill 317. From a photograph taken in 1866.

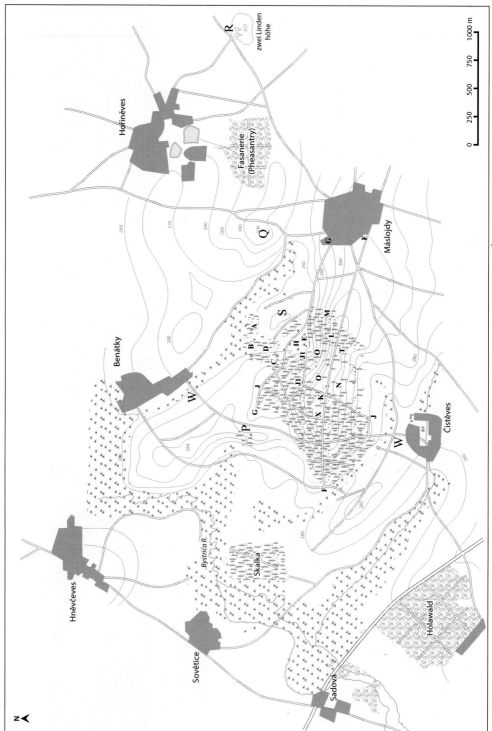

Map 1 The Swiepwald 3rd July 1866.

Foreword

Every year more and more people visit the battlefield of Königgrätz. Recently the number of such visits has increased, primarily due to the efforts of both the Central Association for the Preservation of the Military Memorials of 1866 in Bohemia (Königgrätz) and the local association, the Committee to Preserve the Memorials on the Battlefield of Königgrätz (Sadová), both of whom have greatly assisted visitors. Special attention must be drawn to the 24-metre-high observation platform that has been erected on the crest of Chlum Hill. This fulfills a universally expressed desire, since previously there was no place from which a visitor could obtain an unobstructed view of the entire battlefield. Now this need has been met [in 1996 this platform was replaced by a telecommunications tower with a viewing platform 10 metres higher than the original]. From this observation platform one can observe not only the approach routes and positions of the respective armies (as well as the individual localities and places of importance), but one can also see into the many folds and hollows that score the ground. Thus, the observation platform presents the visitor with the opportunity to completely orientate himself regarding the course of events on that memorable day of 3 July 1866. This will be particularly assisted by the plaque that the Central Association intends to install on the platform.

Let us direct our attention north from the platform, and we shall see about 2,000 paces distant a wood of no great extent, but with a peculiar configuration. This is the famous Swiepwald, whose soil has been soaked with the blood of thousands of brave warriors. Captivated by the sight of these historic woods, the visitor is involuntarily drawn to examine them more closely. Therefore, he descends from the tower and walks through the villages of Lipá and Cistōves to the southern margin of the Swiepwald, where at the entrance to the woods he will encounter the beautiful memorial to Austrian *Feldjäger Bataillon Nr. 8*, the last work of the famous sculptor Tilgner. The memorial depicts an Austrian *Jäger*, who is now the loyal guardian of this once bloody battlefield.

A large number of Austrian and Prussian monuments are located on the perimeter of the woods as well as in the interior, catching the eye and interest of the visitor who will want to learn more about the events associated with them. He will be keen to discover the secrets of the frightful battle that raged here for many hours and demanded such sacrifice and blood. He will search for a detailed description of the struggle in the hope of discovering the particular spot where one or another of his compatriots, his beloved comrades, once performed such heroic deeds. Perhaps the visitor will also want to learn where a member of his own family, or indeed where he himself, may have fought and bled more than three decades ago.

His efforts, however, will remain unrequited, for to date there has been no such account in which one can find all the details of the battle. Both the Austrian and Prussian General Staff studies deal with the battle for the Swiepwald only in broad outline, while the histories of the various formations that took part in the battle only deal with the actions of that particular formation without relating it to the bigger picture. Therefore, by comparing [and contrasting] the accounts in both the Austrian and Prussian histories, these pages will attempt to present the visitor with a more exact and thorough description of the battle.

The hours of bloody struggle for the possession of the Swiepwald consist of a great number of individual actions, many of which will remain veiled due to the nature of forest fighting, while others will attain an exaggerated prominence. An effort will be made here, through the exact reporting of events, to come as close as is possible to the truth of what actually occurred. However, since the author has no sources other than the above-mentioned histories, doubt yet remains as to whether he has been able to achieve his intended goal.

To assist the reader, the more important moments of the fighting have been presented in graphic form ['graphic' in this context means maps and tables]. The description of the organisation of the Austrian and Prussian armies at that time, together with casualty lists, are also appended.

Introduction

Events from 30 June to 2 July 1866

The fighting at Wysokov, Skalitz and Schweinschädel, as well as Alt and Neu Rognitz, had unfortunate results for the Austrian forces, allowing the three corps of the army of the Crown Prince of Prussia that had entered Bohemia by separate routes on the left bank of the upper Elbe to unite.

Especially serious was the defeat of the Austrian 1st Corps and Royal Saxon Corps at Jicin [Gitschin], which resulted in the junction of the Prussian 1st and 2nd Armies. As a result of these actions, the Commander in Chief of the Austrian North Army, *Feldzeugmeister* Benedek, at his Dubenec headquarters, ordered the Austrian Army to withdraw from the position it had taken on the Josefstadt–Salney–Dubenec–Miletin ridge and to concentrate at Königgrätz along the line Nedeliŝt–Chlum–Prím.

In accordance with these orders, the troops left the high ground at Dubenec during the night of 30 June/1 July, and in the course of 1 July (many units only arriving late at night and totally exhausted) arrived at their designated bivouacs. On the morning of 1 July, at 2:30 a.m. the army headquarters rode from Dubenec via Horenoves, Chlum and Nedeliŝt to Königgrätz, giving *Feldzeugmeister* Benedek the opportunity to reconnoitre the ground.

For the Austrian Army, 2 July was a day of relative rest, but reports arriving at the Austrian headquarters throughout the course of day indicated that Prussian advance-guards were already nearby. Consequently, at 11:00 p.m. the headquarters worked out a general disposition of forces for the [impending] battle, dispatching them by courier to the commanders of the [infantry] corps and Cavalry Divisions at 2:00 a.m. on 3 July.[1] *Feldzeugmeister* Benedek anticipated the

---

1   Tr. Note – As a result of the 1859 experience in its war with France, Austria abolished infantry Divisions as too unwieldy. They were replaced by brigades consisting of two infantry regiments (each comprising three battalions, each battalion comprising six companies), one battalion of *Feldjägers* (elite light infantry, also with six companies) and one battery of artillery (eight 4-pounder guns). Four (occasionally five) infantry brigades, together with some light cavalry, additional field artillery and some auxiliary troops constituted an army corps. The Division (that is, a large formation comprising several brigades) was retained for the cavalry. Confusingly, the Austrian infantry did use the term 'division', but this referred to a formation consisting of two companies within a battalion. The Austrian battalion consisted of six, three-ranked companies, each with two *Zugen*, or platoons. Two infantry companies formed a division. The 1st division consisted of the 1st and 2nd Companies of the battalion, the 2nd division consisted of the 3rd and 4th Companies and so on throughout

Prussian attack from the west against the Royal Saxon Corps [on the Austrian left] and there-fore ordered that corps to occupy the heights of Popovic and Tresovic to their left (the south). Cavalry Division Edelsheim formed the extreme left wing[2] of the army. Adjoining the Royal Saxon Corps on the right was the 10th Corps, and on the Chlum Hill, the 3rd Corps, while the 8th Corps was positioned to the rear of the Royal Saxon Corps as its reserve.

The remaining formations merely had to hold themselves in readiness until the Prussians attacked the centre or the right wing, at which point 4th Corps would take position on the high ground between Chlum and Nedelišt and the 2nd Corps would in turn align itself with the 4th Corps on the right, extending to the Elbe as the extreme right wing. The 2nd Light Cavalry Division, the three heavy Cavalry Divisions and the army reserve artillery, together with the 1st Corps and 6th Corps, were designated as the main reserve in the event of a general attack and positioned to the rear of the front line. This reserve remained at the exclusive disposal of the Army Commander [*Feldzeugmeister* Benedek].

Let us now consider the Prussian armies. On the afternoon of 30 June, during his rail journey to Bohemia, King William telegraphed his armies and ordered them to unite and advance without delay toward Königgrätz. On that day (30 June) the Prussian 1st Army was at Jicin, the 2nd Army was on the left bank of the upper Elbe between Arnau and Gradlitz, the Elbe Army was marching toward Libán, and the Guard *Landwehr* Division had arrived at Jungbunzlau. When on 1 July, the Prussian 2nd Army command learned of the withdrawal of the Austrian forces from the Salney–Dubenec–Miletin position, it ordered its I Corps and Cavalry Division Hartmann to cross the Elbe at Neustadtl. I Corps then bivouacked at Ober Praussnitz.

In the afternoon, the advance-guard of the 1st Guards Division (which had bivouacked at Königinhof) also crossed the Elbe and took up position at Doubravic. The advance-guard of the Elbe Army reached Hochveselí. The 1st Army advanced to Horic–Miletin, pushing its leading elements to Cerekvic. On 2 July, the Prussian forces generally undertook no major movements – only the Elbe Army advanced somewhat in order to draw closer to the 1st Army. Its advance-guard reached Smidar.

In King William's headquarters, which arrived at Jicin on the morning of 2 July, it was not yet known that the entire Austrian Army was on the right bank of the Elbe. Rather, it was presumed that its main body was on the far [left] side of the Elbe, between the Adler and Aupa rivers, with its right wing resting on Josefstadt and its left on Königgrätz. On 3 July, the Prussian high command intended to conduct a reconnaissance with the right wing of the Army of the Elbe and take possession of the bridges at Pardubice, so that if the position of the Austrian Army proved too strong and had to be outflanked, then the flanking march could be safely carried out from that direction.

---

the regiment. Typically, an assault might consist of a thin skirmish line formed from (some, not necessarily all) of the *Schutzenzüge*, or rifle platoons of the companies (see footnote 8), followed by an assault column formed from the remainder of the battalion. A Prussian battalion consisted of four companies, but they did not pair their companies in divisions as did the Austrians. In the V Prussian Corps (Von Steinmetz), a regular formation of two companies called a 'half battalion' was used; however, this was not general throughout the Army. Heidrich refers to 'half battalions' but it is unclear if he really means a true 'half battalion' or simply two companies working together.

2   Tr. Note – In the original version Heidrich says 'extreme right wing', which is an obvious error.

From reports received, 1st Army Headquarters assumed that approximately four Austrian corps were on the Bystrice. That being the case, Prince Frederick Charles resolved to attack on the following day and ordered the commander of the Elbe Army to advance on Nechanice as early as possible. [He ordered his own Divisions] to fall in by 2:00 a.m. on the two highways leading from Horic via Sadová and Cerekvic to Königgrätz, and to be ready for action against the position on the Bystrice.

At 9:45 p.m. he informed the Commander of the Prussian 2nd Army [Crown Prince Frederick William] at Königinhof of the impending attack, with the request that he have a corps advance on the right bank of the Elbe as far as Josefstadt to secure the left flank of the 1st Army that was at Gross Jeric and Cerekvic. Having completed his preparations, Prince Frederick Charles dispatched 1st Army's chief of staff (Lieutenant General von Voigts-Rhetz) to the Army high command at Jicin to obtain the King's approval for his plan. The Army High Command, however, took a more critical view of the situation, immediately realising that the main body of the Austrian Army concentrated in front of the Elbe River intended to attack the Prussian centre. Accordingly, it ordered the Crown Prince to immediately advance with all his forces against the right flank of the Austrian Army in support of the 1st Army (this order was dispatched at 12:00 midnight).

On 3 July, the six Divisions of the 1st Army arrived at their appointed places [on the Bystrice] between 4:00 a.m. and 5:00 a.m. At about 6:00 a.m. the 1st Army headquarters received a report from the Elbe Army that it would arrive at Nechanice with 36 battalions between 7:00 and 9:00 a.m. Upon receipt of these reports, Prince Frederick Charles issued orders for the centre to advance.

Let us now see how the Austrian Army was prepared for these combined attacks. It was at 7:30 a.m. (when the sound of gunfire at Sadová reached the Austrian bivouacs) that the different corps took up their positions, exactly as specified in the battle plan. We shall pass over the deployment of the centre corps and focus our attention on the right wing (4th and 2nd Corps). The 4th Corps received its orders between 4:00 and 5:00 a.m. and broke camp at Nedelišt at 8:00 a.m. in order to concentrate between Nedelišt and Chlum. Brigade Brandenstein (4th Corps) was outposted at Másloved. At 3:30 a.m. it received orders to extend its outpost line to the area originally covered by Brigade Wöber [formerly Brigade Kreyssern] of 8th Corps. Thus, at the start of the battle nearly half of Brigade Brandenstein was on the line Horenoves–Benátek.

Because this position (as well as that assigned to 4th Corps between Nedelišt–Chlum) did not provide a view of the ground in front of Másloved and Horenoves [to the north], the commander of the corps, Lieutenant Field Marshal *Graf* Festetics, after conducting a personal reconnaissance, directed the main body of the corps to move to Másloved. When he observed the advance of 4th Corps toward Másloved, the Commander of 2nd Corps, Lieutenant Field Marshal *Graf* Thun, had three of his [four] brigades deploy on the heights south of Horenoves and one on the hill east of Sendrazic (since he would have had to give up the latter without a fight if he had taken up the positions assigned to him in the low ground between Nedelišt and the Elbe).

Before we begin our description of the actual fighting in the woods, we should recount the capture of the village of Cerekvic by the advance-guard of the Prussian 7th Division, a stroke that proved so useful to the Prussian Army. The Prussian 7th Division, commanded by Lieutenant General von Fransecky, marched out at 4:00 p.m. on 1 July from Konecchlum and Kamenic toward Horic. Infantry Regiment 27 formed the advance-guard with its Fusilier Battalion in the lead. The main body of the Division had reached Horic with the advance-guard at Jeric, when the commander of the 27th, Colonel von Zychlinski, received orders to move the advance-guard to Cerekvic. He was to push outposts from there towards Josefstadt and Königgrätz and secure the Bystrice crossings at Cernútek. After an extremely arduous march, but without Austrian interference, the Fusilier Battalion reached Cerekvic at 11:00 p.m. where it took possession of the castle courtyard [by 1866 Schloss Cerekvic was more of a *chateau* than a castle] and positioned patrols at its exits. Colonel Zychlinski vainly endeavoured to obtain more information about the situation, but it proved impossible to communicate with the Bohemian residents of the village. Not until a German-speaking castle servant was found and interrogated by the regimental commander did he learn that the battalion had been inserted like a wedge into the Austrian position, completely enveloped on its left by the line of Austrian outposts that stretched from Horenoves via Vrchovnic to Zelkovic and Zizeloves. The colonel informed his officers of the seriousness of their position and immediately ordered the 11th Company (Captain *Graf* Finkenstein) to take post on the road to Josefstadt, the 12th Company (Captain Bergfeld) on the road to Königgrätz, and the 10th Company (Captain Westernhagen) to remain on the square in front of the castle as support. The 9th Company (Captain von Buddenbrock) was left behind to hold the castle itself. In accordance with these orders, the 11th Company took position at the hunting lodge in front of Cerekvic, posting a piquet on the road toward Benátek at the point where it turned toward Hnevcoves. The 12th Company covered the crossing over the Bystrice southwest of Cerekvic with an outpost and the rest of the company took position 100 paces to its rear.

As a result of the inquiries instituted in the castle, Colonel Zychlinsky dispatched a mounted orderly to divisional headquarters to report a large Austrian encampment at Lipá, as well as the passage of heavy Austrian troop traffic (all arms) through Cerekvic earlier that day. On the outposts, Captain *Graf* Finkenstein concerned himself with obtaining definite information regarding the enemy. Accordingly, at 5:00 a.m. in the morning of 3 July he sent a patrol toward Zelkovic, but it ran into an Austrian *Feldjäger* detachment (presumably from the 24th *Feldjäger* Battalion of Brigade Wöber, 8th Corps) and had to pull back. Somewhat later, Captain *Graf* Finkelstein undertook a reconnaissance ride towards Benátek, from whence an Austrian infantry detachment was just moving out against the Prussian outposts of the 11th Company (which subsequently pulled back). The captain then brought his company up, sending one platoon into the woods east of the road in order to attack the enemy's right flank, or even to cut him off completely. As the skirmish line (which the rest of the company followed) left the woods and passed over a gentle knoll, one gun from an Austrian battery positioned on the slope near Vrchovnic opened fire. The shell burst among the riflemen, drilling right through a Fusilier, who sank to the ground without a sound. This direct hit gave the Prussians an even greater respect for the Austrian artillery than they had hitherto.

That cannon shot served as an alarm signal, for large Austrian infantry detachments immediately appeared at Vrchovnic and Horenoves, as well as at Másloved and Benátek, and a cavalry troop moved out from Horenoves toward Benátek (this may have been the half squadron of the 8th Uhlan Regiment under *Rittmeister Graf* Stockau that had been sent to reconnoitre). In the meantime, the Prussian skirmish line proceeded farther, taking up a position behind a rise in the ground from where it exchanged fire with the numerous Austrian patrols that had hurried there, as well as firing on the above-mentioned cavalry, which then withdrew. However, the Prussian soldiers had to fall back quickly since they were in danger of being enveloped by the enemy.

At the same time as Austrian shells from Vrchovnic, and from a battery that had just set up by the Swiepwald, began to land in the skirmish line, Captain *Graf* Finkenstein fell back with his company to the southeast corner of the woods, and from his vantage point became convinced that significant Austrian forces were concentrated on the plateau opposite.

The emergence of Prussians from the woods was also observed by a ten-man patrol from the Austrian 12th Infantry Regiment [IR 12 Archduke William] under Lieutenant Fuhrmann. Proceeding from Chlum toward Horenoves at about 3:00 a.m. Lieutenant Fuhrmann noticed individual Prussian infantry emerging from the Cerekvic woods, looking around, and then disappearing again. Since he felt that his patrol was too weak to advance any further, he pulled back to the bivouac at Másloved at around 4:00 a.m. and reported this important information. Between 6:00 and 7:00 a.m. stronger Prussian patrols were in evidence, prompting the 2nd Battalion IR 12 to occupy Benátek. When no Prussian attack followed however, the battalion was pulled back again to the bivouac at Másloved.

The 3rd Battalion IR 12 set up outposts, the 7th division [Companies 13 and 14] under Captain Opitz between Horenoves and the Swiepwald, and the 9th division [Companies 17 and 18] in the northern part of the Swiepwald itself.

During the day, Prussian troops were observed moving between the woods south of Cerekvic. Patrols that were sent out toward Benátek also ran into Prussian patrols (mostly in the villages), whereupon the latter always fell back. The 12th Company Pr. F/27 (which was on the right) began to patrol actively at daybreak. A party of four men made it into a village (presumably Cernútek) that had not yet been evacuated by the residents. As the patrol entered a house, a squad of Austrian *Feldjägers* suddenly appeared round a street corner. The Prussians fired several shots at them from a window, killing one. The *Feldjägers* fell back, as did the Prussians, bringing with them the fallen *Jäger*'s hat and rifle as trophies. At 6:00 a.m. the Fusilier Battalion was reinforced by the 3rd Squadron of the Prussian 10th Hussars that had arrived in Cerekvic. At 7:00 a.m. a troop under First Lieutenant von Heister was dispatched to establish contact with the 8th Division, in the process of which two *Jägers* of the Austrian 34th *Feldjäger* Battalion were captured and taken to Cerekvic. Statements from the *Jägers* that they belonged to [Brigade Procházka] Austrian 3rd Corps (which was bivouacked at Lipá) were immediately reported back.

Colonel Zychlinski spent an extremely anxious night, for the situation of his detachment was perilous. Early the next morning, and for the rest of the day, he remained by the statue of Saint John in the castle chapel (from which he had an excellent view of the Austrian positions), watching their movements closely and sending his reports back to Division headquarters.

At 8:00 a.m. the 2nd Battalion that had been sent as reinforcements from Trebovetic arrived, significantly improving the detachment's uncomfortable situation. Precautionary measures were completed and the castle readied for defence. At about noon, Lieutenant General Fransecky showed up in Cerekvic to access the situation personally. He climbed the church tower with Colonel Zychlinski (from where he had a good view of the Chlum plateau) and, after satisfying himself that everything was in order and that the position at Cerekvic was a strong one, made the decision not to pull back the detachment. Soon after the arrival of the 2nd Battalion, the outpost companies (the 11th and 12th) were reinforced with the 9th and 10th, while the 2nd Battalion stayed back as castle garrison. At 2:00 p.m. Captain *Graf* Finkenstein sent a platoon under Lieutenant von Dobeller to discover whether Horenoves was strongly held, but they were soon forced back by Austrian patrols that appeared everywhere. At 3:00 p.m. the Fusilier Battalion was relieved by the 2nd Battalion, a move noted by the Austrian outposts.

Colonel von Zychlinski (who was still extremely concerned about his detachment) was reassured when in the afternoon Lieutenant von Rundstedt of the Guard Hussars informed him that the advance-guard of the Guards Corps was at Doubravic. On his return, Lieutenant von Rundstedt ran into a four-man Austrian cavalry patrol, which he and his two companions were able to outrun, making it safely back to Doubravic.

During the night of 2/3 July the situation at Cerekvic became very uncomfortable, shots were exchanged between the opposing outposts and a light rain drizzled down throughout. As early morning dawned, the action showed no sign of letting up (units of the Prussian 7th Division had been engaged at Cerekvic since 2:30 a.m.).

We will see that the prompt occupation and holding of the village of Cerekvic secured for the Prussians an extremely valuable base that would prove to be of inestimable value during the ensuing battle.

Configuration of the Swiepwald on 3 July 1866[1]

The Swiepwald is irregular in outline, stretching about 2,000 paces from east to west, and about 1,000 paces from north to south. It covers the crest and both slopes of a ridge that stretches from Másloved to the Bystrice. The most elevated parts of the ridge consist of two almost equally high knolls: the western one (Hill 332 K[2]) is nearly at the centre of the wood, while the eastern one (Hill 328 L) is towards its eastern edge. These hills are comparable in elevation to the other commanding heights in the area. The northern slope is steeper than the southern one, both are dissected by many gullies and the foot of the southern slope is boggy.

In 1866 the wood was cut into several parts by the Benátek–Cistōves road [W–W] and by the roads heading west from Másloved [G–G & F–F] as well as by the tracks (*Durchschlag*) [J–J] [see footnote 3] stretching from south to north. Adjoining the main part of the wood, to the north of the road that extends from Másloved [G–G] were three separate sectors A, B, C, which were the most hotly contested points.[3] The western C and central B sectors (which

---

1   Tr. Note – The terrain of the Swiepwald has changed little since 1866, our editor Gerry Henry's first-hand description is extremely helpful here. 'The spine road (in reality, there are no roads in the Swiepwald, track is a better and more accurate description) which runs along the ridgetop east to west from Másloved is roughly metaled and substantial enough to take wheeled vehicles, for example, carts carrying timber, but it is unmetalled past the turn to Cistowes. The *Tiefenlinie* is a narrow depression 20–30 metres wide in places, with a stream running down the middle; marshy and low lying it would not have been planted with trees, but we can fairly assume there would have been some undergrowth. The sunken meadow lies at the bottom of a steep (in places precipitate) slope, dropping from the plateau that lies to the northwest of Másloved. Now lightly overgrown, its margins slightly blurred by saplings, it is still a substantial clearing. The conifers on the knoll (which lies towards the northeastern edge of the meadow) have been replaced by deciduous trees. The meadow itself is boggy (what we would call a water meadow) and drains into the *Tiefenlinie*. Troops in the sunken meadow could not see beyond its perimeter (the slope in places is as much as 5 metres high) and could not themselves be seen.'

2   Ed. Note – The author is inconsistent in his references regarding the elevation of this western knoll K. On the map it is marked 332, a few paragraphs further on it is 337. I have corrected this and refer to it throughout simply as Hill K.

3   Tr. Note – There is ambiguity in the text in references to the central sector B, which is complicated by the fact that in this description of the terrain it states that 'the part of the woods that jutted out toward Másloved M were mostly pole sized trees … whereas the western C and central sectors B … consisted of tall conifers'. For the most part the sector in the centre B, is referred to as 'the central sector'. However, in that part of the text describing the actions of the Prussian 66th Infantry Regiment, it is referred to as 'the pole woods', presumably because in both of the regimental histories

consisted of tall conifers) were separated by a depression D running north–south [described as the *Tiefenlinie*; see footnote 3] towards which both sectors, especially the central one B, dropped steeply. The eastern sector A (the so-called 'Havranec', or 'raven's head') was positioned at right angles to the northern point of the central sector B and dropped steeply off toward the north. This sector consisted of tall oaks with thick undergrowth. The linear depression D [*Tiefenlinie*] that lies between the western and central sectors broadened towards the south to become a sunken meadow E [see footnote 3] bounded on the east by a wave-shaped rise. In the [northeast] of the sunken meadow was a low knoll H covered with tall conifers. The earlier mentioned *Durchschlag* [J–J] began at the angle of the woods that jutted towards Cistōves (to the south), continued north over the western knoll (Hill K) and then (with several branches [J1–J1] that run eastwards towards the sunken meadow) ended at the northern margin where it met the track [G–G]. Those parts to the [north] and west of these tracks [J & J1] consisted primarily of tall growing woods, for the most part fir and oak, with and without undergrowth. The road west from Másloved [F–F] ran along the crest of the ridge and over both hills L and K. On either side of the road the ground fell away, steeply to the north, less so to the south. The slope that extended to the north O (which is about 550 paces wide) had been cleared, whereas only the western end N (about 350 paces wide) of the southern slope that dropped toward Cistōves had been cleared. The eastern end of the southern slope T was covered with saplings.[4] On the cleared slopes O and N, on which there was extremely low, new growth, the trunks of the felled trees (referred to as 'cordwood') were stacked in hundreds of piles. The woods that jutted out toward Másloved M consisted mostly of pole-sized trees.[5]

Bordering the western edge of the tracks [J–J–J1] were tall-growing fir trees, visible from the east and south as a tall, dark wall, which rose far above the young woods to the east.

The eastern and southern margins of the woods were fringed by several rows of fruit trees, such that there was no sharply defined border. The two roads leading into the woods from Másloved, and those leading toward Cistōves, Lipá and Chlum, were often sunken in places (but not in the woods themselves). Southwest of Benátek was a small, isolated wood P, separated by about 350 paces from the northern point of the Swiepwald. Northwest of Másloved is Hill 304 Q. Southeast of Horenoves is Hill 317 R – the hill of the Two Linden Trees. Northeast of the sunken meadow, below the Havranec, is Hill 262 S. West of Hill K, to the north and south of the Másloved road [F–F], is a clearing X. It is entirely possible this clearing was larger and more extensive than Heidrich's map suggests.

of the 66th Infantry Regiment that sector is always referred to as 'the pole woods'. As soon as Heidrich moves on from the references to the Prussian 66th Infantry Regiment, he reverts to calling sector B the central sector.

4   Tr. Note – The forestry term '*Schonung*', which I translate as 'new forest plantation' or the like, refers to fenced off areas of the woods with stands of young trees.

5   Tr. Note – The German forestry term '*Stangenholz*', which I translate as 'pole woods' has a very specific meaning. It is, according to Düden (see bibliograpgy) the stage of development following the young tree stage (*Jungholz*) in which the individual trunks have reached a specified diameter and the lower branches have already been removed.

Small wood marked P on map

The village of Benatek and the northern edge of the Swiepwald.
(Taken from the high ground between Hnevcoves and the road from Benatek to Cerevice, looking south)

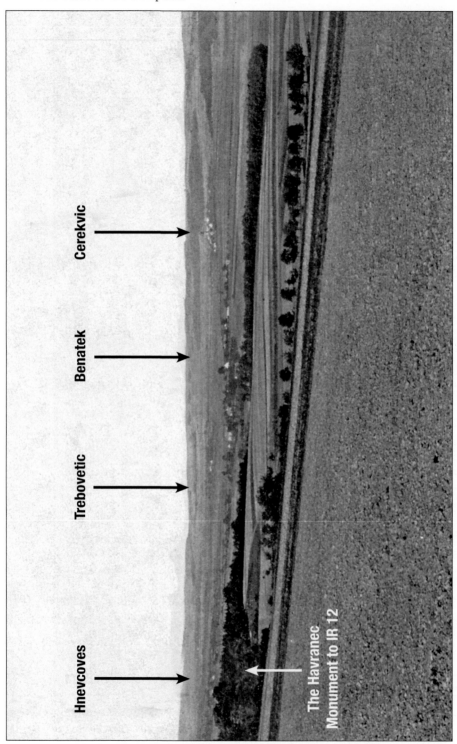

Northeastern part of the Swiepwald and the havranec (crow's head).
(Taken from west of Maslowed)
Battleground of the 2nd & 27th Austrian Feld-Jaegers, and IR 12 & IR 57.

Section I

Events from 7:00 a.m. to 10:00 a.m. in the Morning. Fighting of the Brigades Brandenstein and Appiano

At about 7:00 a.m. on 3 July, the advance-guard of the Prussian 7th Division, consisting of three battalions of the 27th Infantry Regiment, the Fusilier Battalion of the 67th, the 3rd Squadron of the 10th Hussar Regiment and the 4-pdr Battery Rausendorf set off towards Benátek. Since it was known that Benátek was held by the Austrians, the advance-guard marched to the cross-roads south of the Cerekvic woods, where the 4-pdr Battery Rausendorf took position on the hill north of Benátek and fired on the Austrian battery that had gone into action on the high ground west of Másloved. The Hussar squadron took position on the left wing. The 27th then advanced towards Benátek, while the Fusilier Battalion of the 67th swung off to the left and headed toward Horenoves (from whence, however, it came under fire from the Austrian 27th *Feldjäger* Battalion). Thereupon the Fusilier Battalion was immediately re-directed towards the right by Lieutenant General von Fransecky, who did not want to extend his left wing that far. As the three batteries that were still with the main body of the Division passed through Cerekvic, they received orders to move forward to support Battery Rausendorf, which they did, joining the firing line east of the Cerekvic–Benátek road.

Benátek was only held by a single Austrian company (the 7th) of II/IR 26 *Grand Duke Michael* [Brigade Brandenstein, 4th Corps].[1] Upon the approach of superior forces, this company fell back to the northern margin of the Swiepwald, where it linked up with the 8th Company of its own regiment. The Fusilier Battalion Pr. 27 captured Benátek, the 9th Company (under Captain Buddenbrock) occupied the little patch of woods P southwest of the village, while the other three Fusilier companies deployed east of Benátek. Fusilier Battalion Pr. 67 bypassed

---

1   Tr. Note – The reader should be aware that there were several units on both sides bearing the same number. The Austrian Brigade Brandenstein had Infantry Regiment No. 26 (hereafter referred to as IR 26 *Großfürst* Michael). The Prussians had a Regiment Pr. 26 in their 7th Division. The Austrian Brigade Brandenstein included the 27th *Feldjäger* Battalion, while the Prussian 7th Infantry Division included the 27th Infantry Regiment. One of the two battalions that the Prussian 8th Infantry Division sent to support the 7th Division in the Swiepwald was the Magdeburg *Jäger* Battalion Nr. 4. On the Austrian side, Brigade Appiano of the 3rd Army Corps included the Austrian 4th *Feldjäger* Battalion. The shorthand notation we have employed throughout should reduce any confusion.

the village and took up a position further to the east, behind a hill. During their approach, the Prussian battalions suffered seriously from the fire of the Austrian batteries at Másloved (4th Corps) and at the Skalka woods (3rd Corps).

The two Musketeer battalions of the 27th followed the two battalions of the advance-guard [the Fusilier Battalions Pr. 27 and Pr. 67], the 1st Battalion deploying to the right and the 2nd to the left of the 9th Fusilier Company [which was in the small wood P] facing the northwestern edge of the Swiepwald. By now it was 8:00 a.m. Four Prussian battalions stretched in a broad arc around the northern and northwestern margin of the Swiepwald awaiting the approach of the main body of the Division (the 26th and 66th infantry regiments and the two Musketeer Battalions of the 67th).

The 1st Squadron (*Rittmeister* Humbert) of the 10th Pr. Hussar Regiment, maintained contact with the 8th Division, which was approaching [from the west] via Sovetic. The other three squadrons and the somewhat later arriving combined Cavalry Brigade Bismarck (3rd Uhlans and 12th Dragoons) covered the left flank toward Horenoves.

While the main body of the Prussian 7th Division deployed from column of march to battle formation at Benátek, the advance-guard maintained a brisk fire against those Austrians lining the [northern] edge of the woods. Initially, the Prussian 7th Division was faced only by [the Austrian] Brigade Brandenstein of 4th Corps, which was positioned south of Másloved astride the road to Nedelišt. At that time the 2nd Battalion of IR 26 was in the Swiepwald, and five companies of the 27th *Feldjäger* Battalion and the 1st Battalion of IR 26 were in and near Horenoves. The latter battalion had been employed since 9:30 a.m. in covering the guns of the batteries of the Austrian 2nd Corps, which was positioned on the hill southeast of Horenoves (Hill 317 R), the so-called '*Tummelplatz*' [described as an equine exercise area, or *manège*]. The northwestern part of the Swiepwald was also held from the start by the 1st and 2nd Battalions of the Austrian IR 62 *Archduke Henry* of Brigade Appiano, 3rd Corps. [The 1st Battalion dispositions are as follows.] The wooded sector southwest of Benátek was held by the 3rd Company, the part of the Swiepwald that jutted out to the northwest was held by the 4th Company, and the 1st and 2nd Companies were dispersed to the east of the 4th Company. The 5th and 6th Companies (that is, the 3rd division) remained in reserve behind the four mentioned above. [The 2nd Battalion dispositions are as follows.] The 9th, 10th, 11th, and 12th Companies (the 5th and 6th divisions) were positioned at the western border of the woods, while the 7th and 8th Companies (the 4th division) formed the battalion reserve.

At this point (between 6:00 a.m. and 7:00 a.m.), Brigade Appiano was established in a position north of Cistōves, to which it had been assigned by its own corps command the previous day. The other elements of the brigade, the 2nd and 3rd Battalions of IR 46 *Sachsen-Meiningen*, as well as the 3rd Battalion of IR 62, were positioned at the southern edge of the Swiepwald in two lines. The brigade battery (Nr. 3/III) was on some higher ground northwest of Cistōves, facing towards the Bystrice. Adjoining this battery on the left was the 4th *Feldjäger* Battalion, and on the right, in the low ground by the woods, the 1st Battalion of IR 46. The battery now commenced firing on the advance-guard of the Prussian 7th Division.

By 7:30 a.m., the battery of the Austrian Brigade Brandenstein [4th Corps] was already in position on high ground beside the crossroads west of Másloved, covered by a half squadron of the 7th Hussars. At about 8:30 a.m. it was joined by the two horse artillery batteries (Nrs. 7/IV and 8/IV from the 4th Corps Artillery Reserve) and opened fire on the Prussian columns. [As far as the remainder of the brigade was concerned] the Austrian 3rd Battalion IR 12 *Archduke*

Wilhelm and the 3rd Battalion IR 26 were *en route* to the Swiepwald, while the 1st and 2nd Battalions IR 12 had been dispatched to support the 4th Company, 27th *Feldjäger* Battalion under Captain *Baron* Gorizutti, which had been positioned on the hill (Hill Q) between the high road [to Bürglitz] and the road to Benátek.

The other three brigades of 4th Corps as well as the artillery reserve (as mentioned earlier in the introduction) moved out of their bivouac around Nedelišt at about 8:00 a.m. in a northerly direction. Brigade Fleischhacker took the lead, but it was soon directed [westwards] toward Cistôves, while Brigades Archduke Josef and Poeckh continued to advance toward Másloved. The corps artillery reserve was placed at the head of the column of march at the very beginning, thus making it possible for the previously mentioned two horse artillery batteries to go to the support of the battery of Brigade Brandenstein in such timely fashion. The other four batteries remained in reserve behind the hill, covered by the 7th Hussars.

It was probably about 8:00 a.m. when the main body of the Prussian 7th Division arrived at Benátek and deployed for action in the low ground north of the village. At the same time, the four advance-guard battalions launched their attack on the north and northwestern borders of the Swiepwald. The Austrian batteries at Másloved, Cistôves and the Skalka woods opened fire on the attackers, however the soggy meadow ground interfered with the explosion of the shells, thereby reducing what would otherwise have been significant losses. Of the Prussian batteries, the 4th 12-pdr Battery (Notz) [smooth bore] and the 1st 6-pdr Battery (Kühne) [rifled] opened fire from the hill southeast of Benátek. The first battery soon had a gun dismounted.

Three companies (the 10th, 11th, and 12th) Pr. F/27th advanced southeast of Benátek, directing their advance toward the re-entrant angle on the northern border of the woods [presumably where the track G–G meets the western border of the western sector C]. The 1st Battalion and the 9th Company Pr. F/27 advanced to the west of the Benátek–Cistôves road, and the 2nd Battalion Pr. 27 to the east.

Shortly before this attack (by order of Brigadier Appiano), the two Austrian battalions of IR 62 withdrew from the northwestern part of the Swiepwald to join the rest of their brigade at Chlum in accordance with the dispositions made for the battle. General Appiano believed that the time had come for his battalions to fall back since the advance-guard of the Prussian [7th] Division had halted its advance toward the woods (after deploying in the meadow south of Benátek) and seemed to be limiting itself to a firefight. He was also concerned for his right flank and its exposed battery, which had already been engaged for some time, with four guns facing north and the other four facing west. So it was, that when the Prussian advance-guard attacked, there were only two Austrian companies (the 7th and 8th IR II/26) defending the northern edge of the woods. These had taken cover in a ditch and put up a determined resistance. The 9th Company IR II/26 (which had been dispatched by the battalion command as support) took position on their left.

The three battalions of the Prussian 27th IR hurried across the meadow between Benátek and the Swiepwald and were able to push into the weakly defended margin of the woods with the loss of two officers and 40 men. Here they quickly regrouped and resumed their advance. Now, however, the hard work began for the Prussians.

The history of the Prussian 27th IR describes the ensuing action in the following words:

> All three companies resumed their advance at about the same time, into the dark, myste-
> rious, unfamiliar woods, but also into a fearsome, massed shellfire, the noise of which rose

to a deafening thunder. Trees exploded with a sharp crack, branches were sheared off, whole tree trunks torn into flying splinters. In the leaves above, rockets buzzed and hissed. Rifle and musket bullets of a generally unseen enemy flew from the concealment of the undergrowth with a whispering whistle. In many places the woods were so thick that the advancing companies were brought to a halt. Nearly everywhere organisation broke down and command from above was almost impossible. Contact with individual detachments was lost. Patrols were sent to find adjoining units, but in vain. Men called and whistled to let each other know of their presence. Here and there bugles were even sounded, but it only heightened the confusion … orders were given without being understood, others were heard without anyone knowing who had given them resulting in unintended changes of direction, which themselves made any attempt at unified operations all the more difficult.

The 10th, 11th and 12th Companies of Pr. F/27 advanced from the edge of the woods towards the eastern part of the tall timber,[2] coming under heavy fire from the three above-mentioned companies of IR II/26. The three Prussian companies were able to bypass the three Austrian companies, forcing the latter to fall back. When the Austrians reached the far edge of the woods, they linked up with the other three companies of their battalion, whose commander, Major Barisani, had been ordered to push the [Prussians] back. This counterattack did indeed bring the battalion temporary possession of the [northern] boundary of the woods, but only briefly as the threat to its left flank soon made it retreat. Now reinforced by the 3rd Battalion of its own regiment, the 2nd Battalion IR 26 (which had fallen back nearly to the crest of the ridge) was ordered to recapture its former position by Lieutenant Field Marshal Mollinary (who had just arrived). However, as we shall later see, the self-sacrificing endeavours of these two battalions was in vain.

The three Prussian Fusilier companies thus overcame the resistance of the Austrian units that were facing them, as well as the [physical] impediments to their movement. They continued their advance and soon reached (though with heavy losses) the edge of the tall timber. The 10th Company Pr. F/27 (Captain von Westernhagen) got as far as the crossroads of the track [J–J] with the spine road leading from Másloved [F–F]. The 11th Company Pr. F/27 took position behind its left flank, while the 12th Company under Captain von Bergfeld emerged from the border of the tall timber and found cover behind the nearest stacks of cordwood. The fronts of the companies faced east and southeast, respectively; however, they could advance no further, for here they came up against the 2nd and 3rd Battalions IR 26, whose heavy fire stopped any further progress. It was an emphatic 'Halt!' and it resulted in an extremely bloody firefight. Alone in the face of reinforcements arriving from the main body of the Prussian 7th Division, pinned in front by the above mentioned three Fusilier companies and under murderous fire, the two Austrian battalions [IR 26] had to fall back, partly into that area of the woods jutting toward Másloved M (which was now occupied by the 3rd Battalion IR 12), and partly into the open fields beyond.

Let us now turn our attention to the advance of the two Musketeer battalions and the 9th Fusilier Company of the Prussian 27th IR from the edge of the woods to the interior. Before the two Austrian battalions of IR 62 had withdrawn from the Swiepwald (by order of Brigadier

2   Tr. Note – The forestry term 'Hochwald', I translate here as 'tall timber'.

Appiano), the 4th division (7th and 8th Companies), which formed the 2nd Battalion's reserve, was assigned by the Brigade General Staff Officer (Captain Hegedüs) to cover Horse Artillery Batteries 7/VIII and 8/VIII, which had been sent forward to the Cistōves Hill. Accordingly, the 4th division moved out of the southern edge of the woods (west of Cistōves) and took up its assigned position.

The commander of the regiment, Colonel Czermak, led the 1st Battalion IR 62, along with the other two divisions of the 2nd Battalion, out of the woods to a position behind the Másloved–Cistōves sunken road. Hardly had this movement been completed, however, when Captain Hegedüs arrived with [new orders] from Major General Appiano stating that both battalions were to re-enter the Swiepwald and to hold it at all costs and for as long as possible. [Major General Appiano] had become aware of the attack by the Prussian advance-guard, and the subsequent, ever-increasing intensity of the fighting after the withdrawal of the two battalions from the woods. At the same time, he also sent four companies of the 4th *Feldjäger* Battalion with them. The other two companies were detached to support the 33rd *Feldjäger* Battalion that was in the Skalka woods. However, on arrival they found the 33rd *Feldjägers* [Brigade Procházka, 3rd Corps] in the process of withdrawing and so returned to their own brigade.

Major General Appiano then took the brigade battery and his three remaining battalions to their assigned position at Chlum, leaving the 1st Battalion IR 46 east of Cistōves to cover the troops of his brigade that were fighting in the Swiepwald [should they be forced to retreat].

As a result of the withdrawal of the two battalions of IR 62 from the Swiepwald, the Austrians were placed at a serious disadvantage in that the [right wing of the] attacking Prussian advance-guard (the 1st and 2nd Battalions and the 9th Company Pr. /27) found the northwestern part of the Swiepwald practically unoccupied. Due to the belated nature of their intervention, the two battalions of Brigade Appiano that re-entered the woods were unable to improve the situation. The 2nd Battalion Pr. 27 had already advanced some distance into the woods before it ran into the above-mentioned Austrian battalions. The men of IR 62 advanced against the Prussians in *Divisionsmassen*[3] preceded by a dense line of skirmishers. The 1st Battalion was given as its objective that part of the forest it had formerly occupied, while the 5th and 6th divisions [of the 2nd Battalion] had to follow on the right in support. The part of the woods the 1st Battalion had to cross was comprised of tall timber with thick under-growth, whereas the two divisions of the 2nd Battalion only had to deal with light, man-high undergrowth which hindered their advance less. Because of this, the 1st Battalion effectively vanished from sight after entering the woods and had to make its way laboriously forward, while the 2nd Battalion advanced more rapidly and thereby drew more and more to the right. This resulted in a substantial gap developing between the two battalions as they moved north-west towards the centre of the woods.

---

3   Tr. Note – As described by Herbert Schwarz, the *Divisionsmasse* is an entirely closed-up column, denser than the normal closed-up column. It replaces the two-company division (comprising *two* companies in *two* double ranks, side by side) with *four* half companies, each *four* double ranks deep, again side by side. When the battalion formed in *Divisionsmassenlinie*, the three *Divisionsmassen* were positioned alongside each other with only a few paces interval (*Zwischenraum*) between them, giving a battalion formation eight ranks (four double ranks) deep and six half companies in width (Herbert Schwarz. *Gefechtsformen der Infanterie in Europa durch 800 Jahre* (Munich: Selbstverlag, 1977))

The 4th Feldjäger Battalion, which had suffered some losses from Prussian shrapnel during its advance, moved forward on the left of the 1st Battalion and became engaged in a very costly fight with the 1st Battalion Pr. 27, while the 2nd Battalion IR 62 again ran into the 2nd Battalion Pr. 27, and it too suffered substantial losses from the Prussian *schnellfeuer* [rapid fire]. Both the Austrian 4th *Feldjägers* and the 1st Battalion IR 62 had to fall back to the south-eastern edge of the woods after they were engaged on their right flank by the 9th Company Pr. F/27. In this action the 4th *Feldjägers* lost Captain *Graf* Waldersdorff, one *Oberjäger* and four *Jägers* were killed, as well as Captain Wolf, Lieutenant Kessler and Lieutenant *Baron* Lützow, and another *Oberjäger* and ten *Jägers* were wounded. The two divisions of the 2nd Battalion were not informed of the retreat of the 1st Battalion and the 4th *Feldjägers,* and stormed the crest of the ridge east of the Benátek–Cistöves road despite extremely heavy enemy fire. They achieved short-lived success and forced the enemy back, but in so doing Lieutenants *Baron* Spielmann and Lederhawz both fell. Alone and hard pressed by the Prussians following the withdrawal of the 1st Battalion and the *Feldjägers,* the two divisions had to fall back themselves. They reached the eastern margin of the woods and re-assembled in the Másloved–Lipá sunken road, where they were able to cover those parts of IR 26 that were retreating out of the woods in the same direction. The 4th *Feldjägers* and the 1st Battalion IR 62 passed through the lines of the 1st Battalion IR 46 that was east of Cistöves, then (together with the 4th *Feldjägers*) it [IR 46] marched off to Chlum to join its brigade, leaving the 1st Battalion IR 62 between Cistöves and Lipá.

After entering the woods, the 5th Company Pr. II/27 (Captain Joffroy) kept its right flank on the Benátek–Cistöves road and fought its way (though with painful losses) as far as the road from Másloved (which ran along the crest of the ridge), where a firefight developed in which Captain Joffroy was severely wounded and Lieutenant Zedwitz killed. The 8th Company Pr. II/27 (Captain Kretschmann) kept pace with the 5th Company and advanced on its left flank without, however, achieving the desired contact with the three Fusilier companies (10th, 11th and 12th) of its own regiment. [As a result of this] some Austrians were able to infiltrate the gap between the 8th and 5th Companies Pr. II/27, on one side, and the Fusiliers on the other. This forced the 8th Company Pr. II/27 to deploy one platoon under Lieutenant Diringshofen with its front facing east. The fighting that then developed took a heavy toll in casualties. Every step forward was bought with blood (Lieutenant Balant was severely wounded there).

The riflemen crossed the Másloved road and took cover (south of it); however, they then came under severe pressure from the east. Lieutenant Diringshofen's platoon was able to reach the edge of the tall timber and link up with a platoon of the 10th Company Pr. F/27. Right in front of them was the northern cleared area O, where they came under fire from Austrians who were shooting from behind the piles of cordwood. They also began to suffer significant losses from the intense Austrian shellfire. In the meantime, the other two companies, the 6th and 7th [Pr. II/27], advanced through the woods against relatively weak opposition and joined the 5th Company where the Benátek–Cistöves road crosses the spine road from Másloved, taking significant losses to rifle and shell fire on the way. Lieutenant Hanstein's platoon of the 4th Company [1st Battalion] advanced particularly rapidly. It was not until it reached a clearing east of the Benátek–Cistöves road that it encountered significant resistance (as Lieutenant Hanstein's first-hand account tells us) in the form of the skilled marksmen of the Austrian 4th *Feldjägers* (presumably half of the 2nd Company), who blocked its further progress with heavy, well-aimed fire.

The 1st Company Pr. I/27 (Captain Schramm) secured the right flank and advanced directly along the western edge [of the forest], while the 2nd and 3rd Companies Pr. I/27 followed behind the 4th Company in close order as a half battalion. As mentioned above, [the 1st Battalion] became engaged with the Austrian 4th *Feldjäger* Battalion (which then fell back); however, Lieutenant Hanstein's platoon was unable to break through the *Feldjägers* facing them. It was only when these *Feldjägers* withdrew from their position (to follow the rest of their retreating battalion) that Lieutenant Hanstein and his platoon were able to continue their advance. When they reached the southern margin of the woods (east of the Benátek–Cistōves road) Lieutenant Hanstein's platoon opened up with *schnellfeuer* on the retreating IR 62 and 4th *Feldjägers* however the latter repeatedly stopped, reversed front, and returned their fire.

As the shooting died down, Lieutenant Hanstein's platoon renewed its advance and took up a position behind a rise on the Cistōves meadow (east of the Benátek–Cistōves road). In the meantime, the rest of the 4th Company, along with the 1st, 2nd and 3rd Companies [all Pr. I/27] reached the southern margin of the woods (west of the Benátek–Cistōves road). There they came under heavy fire from the retreating troops, as well as from the 1st Battalion IR 46 (which had been tasked with covering the retreat and had not yet commenced its withdrawal to Chlum) as well as from the 4th division (7th and 8th Companies) IR II/62, which had remained in position after the departure of the two batteries it had been assigned to cover (these batteries were forced to withdraw towards Lipá as the result of heavy enemy rifle fire coming from the woods). The 4th division opened heavy fire on the right flank of the Prussian forces emerging from the woods, however an artillery captain from Brigade Procházka soon ordered them to withdraw as they were blocking the fire of the brigade battery that had taken position about 2,000 paces to the west (at the Sadová–Königgrätz road). Accordingly, they fell back to Chlum. In this fight, Lieutenant Colonel von Sommerfeld and Captain Diets (4th Company Pr. I/27) were both struck down by rifle bullets.

Our attention must now turn to the 9th Company Pr. F/27 (Captain von Buddenbrock), which advanced along the Benátek–Cistōves road, maintaining contact between the 1st Battalion [on the right] and the 2nd Battalion [on the left] Pr. 27. After heavy fighting with the Austrian IR 62 and the 4th *Feldjäger* Battalion, and having suffered heavy losses, the company crossed the Másloved road on the crest of the ridge, where for a time they took position on the southern slope, thereby serving as a link between the 1st and 2nd Battalions Pr. 27, on the one side, and the Fusilier Battalion Pr. 27, on the other. It was 9:45 a.m.

Let us now turn to the northern and eastern part of the woods and follow the course of events there. At the same time as the attack of Pr. 27, the Fusilier Battalion of the 67th was also attacking the Swiepwald, with the northern tip and the Havranec A as their objective. During this attack, the Fusiliers had to cross an open field where they came under fire from the 4th Company of the Austrian 27th *Feldjägers* and the 1st Battalion IR 12, which were positioned on Hill Q. Accordingly, the Fusilier Battalion drew off more to the right, driving before it the weaker part of the Austrian 2nd Battalion IR 26 facing it. Pushing on through the *Tiefenlinie* D, they took possession of the central sector B, with the 9th Company front facing southeast towards Másloved and the 10th and 11th Companies at the northeastern point of the woods front facing northeast.

In the meantime, the 3rd Battalion IR 12 (Austrian), had arrived in that part of the wood designated M. The 8th division (15th and 16th Companies), under Captain Chambaud, reached the northern border of the young tree plantation that covered the steep northern slope of the ridge, ahead of them was the sunken meadow E. The 7th and 9th divisions remained behind in the projecting woods for the time being.

Initially there was no sign of the enemy, but small arms fire (which gradually drew nearer) could be heard from the north. From his commanding position Captain Chambaud saw that Austrian troops (the 1st Battalion IR 12) were advancing from the east [from Hill Q] toward the central sector of the woods B. In order to assist this attack, Captain Chambaud doubled down the slope with [half of] the 15th Company deployed as skirmishers, first to the wooded knoll H in the sunken meadow, and from there to the southern tip of the central sector B.

Once there, however, heavy rifle fire drew his attention to the field beyond, where he saw the Austrian troops (whose attack he had intended to support) in full retreat. Realising that he could not now maintain his position, he led his skirmishers back to the wooded knoll H, upon which the one and a half companies that were following on had firmly established themselves. This manoeuvre had barely been completed when Fusiliers of Pr. 67 appeared on the track at the southern tip of the central sector [G–G]. This was probably the 9th Company, which had advanced to the eastern edge of the central sector during the Austrian attack and, following the defeat of that attack, had pulled back to its former position.

A lively firefight then developed between this Prussian force and [Captain Chambaud's] 8th division at a range of about 200 paces. However, it soon became evident that the Prussians were being constantly reinforced from Benátek, and thus there was no other choice [for the Austrians] than to limit themselves to the defence of the eastern sector of the woods (near Másloved) and prevent the enemy from advancing into it.

In the meantime, the 7th and 9th divisions (13th and 14th, 17th, and 18th Companies IR III/12) had been brought forward and took over this difficult task. The 7th division took position in the border of the woods to the right, the 9th to the left, while the 8th was pulled back and held in reserve behind the left flank in the sunken road that led into the Swiepwald. These two forward divisions resolutely held the edge of the woods and successfully beat back several attempted attacks by smaller enemy units.

Earlier, as the Fusilier Battalion of Pr. 67 advanced toward the Swiepwald, the hill northwest of Másloved [to their left] Q was lightly held by the 4th Company of the Austrian 27th *Feldjäger* Battalion. The skirmishers of the Prussian battalion (whose objective, as mentioned earlier, was the northern tip of the woods) drifted slightly to the east during their advance and thereby ran into the *Feldjägers'* own skirmish line. The *Feldjägers* delayed their advance with heavy fire but were too weak to hold the hill for any length of time against such superior odds. Possession of the hill would have been of great value to the Prussians, not only would it cover their left flank in the Swiepwald, but it would also serve as a strongpoint for an attack on Másloved. Thus, at the very start of the battle the enemy was in danger of driving a wedge between the Austrian 2nd and 4th Corps.

This danger was recognised by Captain Schmedes [General Staff Officer, Brigade Brandenstein], who galloped over to the *Feldjäger* Company (which, threatened by enemy cavalry, had started to form clumps, while simultaneously defending itself against swarms of enemy riflemen climbing towards it from between Horenoves and Benátek) and ordered the company commander, Captain *Baron* Gorizutti, to reinforce the skirmish line and hold the enemy until reinforcements could reach him. Captain Schmedes then galloped back to the brigade area and (after receiving permission from the Brigadier) led the 1st and 2nd Battalions IR 12 to the hill, behind which the 1st Battalion deployed for action in *Divisionsmassenlinie* [see Footnote 3], while the 2nd Battalion remained echeloned on the road in battalion column. The *Feldjäger* skirmish line (which was already in a critical situation due to the enemy's superior numbers) shifted northeast (to the right) and was augmented by skirmishers that had been brought up from IR 12. After a short but extremely lively firefight, the Prussian Fusiliers fell back and so the above-mentioned danger was averted.

Three companies (the 1st, 2nd, and 3rd) of the five companies of the 27th *Feldjäger* Battalion then advanced [from Horenowes] towards Benátek and forced the two enemy batteries (Notz and Kühne) that were positioned southeast of it to withdraw behind the village. However, threatened by cavalry to their right, these three companies soon had to fall back again toward Horenoves, whereupon batteries Notz and Kühne again advanced, followed this time by the two batteries (Nordeck and Rausendorf) that had been left behind on the hill north of Benátek. Initially, the 5th 4-pdr Battery Nordeck advanced through the village to support the infantry attack, unlimbering with one two-gun section south of the village and the other two sections directly east of the village, where the two batteries that had been driven off by the *Feldjäger* later joined them.[4] In the same manner, the 4-pdr advance-guard battery (Rausendorf) advanced through the burning village of Benátek and opened fire (from a position south of the village) on the Austrian batteries near Másloved. Aside from several minor adjustments, the Prussian batteries remained in this position for the rest of the battle until the arrival of the Guards, when they repositioned forward. They lost a total of one officer, 15 men and 27 horses. After the attack of its riflemen on Hill Q was repelled, Fusilier Battalion Pr. 67 shifted farther to the right, that is to the southwest, and as mentioned earlier, pushed into the Swiepwald at its northern tip.

At this point on the Austrian side, the 1st and 2nd Battalions IR 12, along with the 4th Company 27th *Feldjägers*, were ordered to advance [from Hill Q] towards the forest. In the meantime, however, Lieutenant General Fransecky brought up two of *his* battalions (the Fusilier and 1st Battalions Pr. 66) to support the advance-guard. According to the history of the 66th Prussian Infantry Regiment, this took place at about 8:45 a.m. (the same history gives the time the main body of the 13th Infantry Brigade went into battle as 9:00 a.m.).

It turned out, after the four Prussian advance-guard battalions had entered the woods and forced the Austrians facing them to retreat, that the extent of the Swiepwald (which was not marked on the Prussian maps) was quite considerable, so much so that that a large gap opened up between the Fusilier Battalion of Pr. 67 and the westward advancing Pr. 27.

The Fusilier Battalion of Pr. 66 passed the brightly burning village of Benátek and then advanced at the double over the meadow towards the woods, all the while under heavy fire from the Austrian artillery. The soggy ground of the meadow did indeed prevent most of the incoming Austrian shells from exploding, nevertheless, casualties increased significantly. Second Lieutenant Barbenès of the 11th Company was hit in the neck by an entire shell. They also came under heavy rifle fire from the edge of the woods to which individual groups of Austrian troops had returned. Nevertheless, the battalion forced its way into the northern tip. The 11th Company Pr. F/66 (Captain Przychowski) advanced to the southern extremity of the central sector B, passing through two companies (9th and 10th) of Fusilier Battalion Pr. 67 that were positioned there, while the rifle platoon under Lieutenant Platten sought to capture the commanding high ground (that is, the ridge on the far side of the *Tiefenlinie* D) by advancing

---

4   Tr. Note – A Prussian battery had six guns; an Austrian battery had eight.

to its right. The 9th Company Pr. F/66 (*Premier Lieutenant* Gneist) followed the rifle platoon. The 10th and 12th Companies Pr. F/66 took position in the middle of the sector, while the latter company established contact with the 12th Company Pr. F/67, which was fighting in the northeastern corner of the same sector.

The area in which the 1st Battalion IR 12 *Archduke Wilhelm* was initially employed was bounded to the east by the Másloved–Vrchovnic [Bürglitz] road, on the west by sectors A and B of the woods and the sunken meadow E, on the north by the road from Másloved to Benátek, and on the south by the track that branches off from the road [G–G] and runs along the southern edge of the sunken meadow.

Open pasture extended to the north and west of the Másloved–Vrchovnic road, while to the south, along the valley that runs between Hill Q and the steep slope of the Másloved Hill, was an area of cultivated fields approximately 400 paces wide. These fields were broken by several gullies cutting across them and running down into the valley bottom. Of these, the one about 600 paces before the northern sector of the Swiepwald was large enough to provide an extremely suitable [covered] assembly area for attacking the woods. However, due to the open nature of the approach, an attack from here would prove to be extremely costly. The central sector of tall timber B formed the backdrop to the area described above. When it became evident that the Prussians held sector B, the Austrian 1st Battalion IR 12, together with the 4th Company 27th *Feldjägers* (echeloned to the right) advanced along the valley to attack them. The 2nd division IR I/12 (3rd and 4th Companies), under Captain Martini, was held back in reserve; during the attack it was to wait beside the fruit orchard in the valley bottom at the southeastern foot of Hill Q. The 1st and 3rd divisions proceeded by a lateral march into the large gully that cut across the valley floor, strengthening their skirmish line in the meantime.

With the 1st division (Captain Thalmayer) on the right and the 3rd division (Captain Jaksi) on the left, the battalion (commanded by Major Vogel) launched its attack. When it had come to within 250 paces of the enemy, the 10th and 12th Companies, Pr. F/66 and Pr. F/67, opened up with a murderous fire from the edge of the woods, inflicting heavy losses and forcing the battalion to retreat. Nevertheless, one group of attackers [4th Company 27th *Feldjägers*] gained a foothold in the Havranec A and through that came to within a few paces of the pole woods B, that is the central sector (see Configuration, footnote 3). The 12th Company Pr. F/66 was forced back, but its rapid fire made any further advance by the Austrians impossible. The two divisions of IR 12 that were falling back sought cover in a narrow ditch as well as the valley that extended from the Havranec towards the gully [in which they had formed up for the attack]. During this action both division commanders and Lieutenant Pfifferling were severely wounded and there were heavy losses among the men. During the attack the 11th Company Pr. F/66 (Captain Przychowski), which had reached the southern tip of the central sector B, advanced through the sunken meadow and climbed Hill S, thereby outflanking the attacking Austrians. *Oberlieutenant*[5] Banhans of the 6th Company IR I/12 spotted the danger, however, and sent a swarm of skirmishers forward against the Prussian company. The Prussians, who were also taking flanking fire from the Austrian 3rd Battalion IR 12 and the 3rd Battalion IR 26 [in that part of the wood designated M], as well as coming under increasingly heavy shellfire, now had to fall back to a position in the sunken meadow. At the same time, hereabouts, Major General

---

5   Tr. Note – The author uses the spelling '*Oberlieutenant*', rather than the more familiar *Oberleutnant*.

Brandenstein fell from his horse after being hit by two rifle bullets and had to be carried from the battlefield.

[As stated previously] the 4th Company of the Austrian 27th *Feldjägers* assaulted the northern tip of the woods and forced their way into it but had to fall back with substantial losses (three officers and 60 men) before superior enemy forces. The 10th and 12th Companies Pr. F/66 then launched a counterattack [out of the woods] into the open ground. That, too, miscarried, costing the life of Lieutenant Wintzingerode of the 12th Company.

At 9.00 am, of the four batteries of the Austrian corps artillery reserve that stood in readiness east of Másloved (covered by the 7th Hussars), Battery Nr. 5/IV positioned west of the village and Rocket Battery Nr. 11/IV at the northwest of the village opened fire. Batteries 9/IV and 10/IV went into action later at about 10:00 a.m. the same time as the attack of Brigade Poeckh. Meanwhile, Battery Nr. 3/IV of that brigade, as well as Battery Nr. 4/IV of Brigade Archduke Josef also joined the line of the Corps Artillery Reserve.

While the two divisions of the Austrian IR 12 that had been repelled prepared for a new attack and the Fusiliers of the [Prussian] 66th began to regroup [after their abortive counter-attack], the 1st Battalion Pr. 66 arrived in the central sector of the woods B and immediately took up the following positions. The 2nd Company under Captain Westernhagen deployed in line south of the Havranec before the pole woods, alongside the 12th [Fusilier] Company. The 3rd Company under Captain Hering positioned itself somewhat closed-up at the northwestern corner of the Havranec behind a 1.5-metre-high, wall-like embankment. The 4th Company under Captain Werder took position to the left on the meadow slope, where the 12th Company Pr. F/67 was also located. The 1st Company Pr. I/66 under Captain Rauchhaupt remained in the pole woods as reserve.

Austrian *Feldjägers* were then seen advancing across the meadow and seemed to be heading for the 3rd and 4th Companies [of Pr. I/66] and the 12th Company Pr. F/67. This could only have been the 3rd division of the 27th *Feldjägers*, which had become separated from its own battalion (during the advance of the 1st division and one company of the 2nd division) and was now marching toward the Swiepwald. This assault was repelled by rapid fire; despite this, however, individual groups seem to have reached the Havranec A and established themselves there.

At the same time, the 1st and 3rd divisions of IR I/12 (Austrian) completed their regrouping and were again sent forward [from their covered position in the valley] against the pole woods. Here they came up against the 2nd Company Pr. II/66, which was deployed in line and strongly supported by the 12th [Fusilier] Company of the same regiment. In the face of this devastating fire, [the Austrians] were again forced to retreat. This attack failed because it was launched by an exhausted, depleted formation without the assistance of the 2nd division which remained in reserve. That division, however, could not be brought up in time to join the assault because it had been shifted from its original position southwest of Hill Q (where it was suffering badly from enemy fire) to a more sheltered location. The 6th Company of the regiment therefore had to conduct a lengthy firefight entirely on its own.

Following the repulse of that attack, Captain Przychowski returned to Hill S with the 11th and 12th Companies Pr. F/66 and some 80 men of the Fusilier Battalion of the Prussian 67th IR, and from there fired on those Austrian that were withdrawing toward Másloved.

The 2nd, 3rd, and 4th Companies Pr. I/66 that were beside the pole woods were hard-pressed by the fire of the Austrian *Feldjäger* that had settled into the Havranec. In an attempt to alleviate the situation, the 2nd Company sent its rifle platoon under Lieutenant Breymann directly against the Havranec, while at the same time the 4th Company sent its rifle platoon (as well as the 8th Platoon) in a flanking attack. Lieutenant Breymann immediately launched a bayonet charge but was felled by three bullets before he took more than a few steps, as were a large number of his riflemen. The remnants of the platoon then attempted to return to their original positions.

Since the 2nd Company Pr. I/66 was under heavy fire both from its front and from the cleared northern slopes O to its right flank and rear, the regimental commander of the Prussian 66th IR, Colonel von Blankensee, ordered that the Austrians be driven from these slopes. Accordingly, the 3rd Company Pr. I/66 was sent there, advancing through the pole woods and the *Tiefenlinie*. At the same time, the 11th and 12th Companies Pr. F/66, along with 80 men of the Fusilier Battalion of the 67th IR, advanced up the middle of the slope towards the crest of the ridge. The 10th Company was left behind in the western sector of the pole woods C in reserve. The 1st Company Pr. I/66, which had formerly been in reserve, moved to the position in front of the pole woods (where the 2nd Company had originally been). The 2nd Company now moved farther towards the Havranec A.

According to the history of the Prussian 66th Infantry Regiment, the other four battalions of the main body of the Prussian 7th Division joined the battle at 9:00 a.m. These were brought forward at about 8:45 a.m. from their position behind Benátek and with the 1st and Fusilier Battalions of Pr. 26, bypassed the village on its eastern side and climbed the hill, while the 2nd Battalion Pr. 26 and the 2nd Battalion Pr. 66 marched through the village and advanced across the meadow in front of it. During their advance, the battalions came under heavy fire from the Austrian batteries. The 1st and 2nd Battalions of the 26th received so much flanking fire from the cornfields east of the Benátek–Másloved road that each battalion directed a platoon of skirmishers in that direction. The skirmishing platoon of the 2nd Battalion soon returned, whereas that of the 1st Battalion, under Lieutenant von Platen, did not return to its battalion during the battle. It became engaged with skirmishers from the Austrian 27th *Feldjägers* in an ongoing firefight and was later driven back into the northern part of the forest.

The battalions reached the [northern] edge of the woods at nearly the same time, whereupon the 2nd Battalion Pr. 66 advanced farther south into the sunken meadow and was placed in reserve for the time being. In the meantime, the 4th Company and some of the 3rd Company Pr. I/66, along with the 12th Company Pr. F/67, drove out the weak Austrian detachments that held the Havranec and then charged to the eastern edge of the wood where they came under heavy fire from [the 3rd Battalion] IR 12. However, the 2nd Company Pr. I/66, which was positioned a bit to the right, threw these Austrians back, assisted by the Fusilier Battalion of the 26th, which (advancing from Benátek) struck the Austrians in [their] right flank. In the meantime [as stated earlier], those Prussians that were fighting in the *Tiefenlinie* were hard-pressed by continuous fire directed at their flank and rear from the wooded ridge behind them, where the third battalions [from IR 12 and IR 26] were positioned. Yet more companies, the 2nd and 4th of Pr. I/66, were sent against the ridge, which was already under attack by the 9th, 11th, and 12th Companies Pr. F/66, as well as most of the 3rd Company Pr. I/66.

The latter two companies [the 2nd and 4th Pr. I/66] advanced towards the slope through the line of the *Tiefenlinie*, passing through the Fusiliers of Pr. 67 that were at the southern corner of the pole woods, and the 11th and 12th Companies Pr. F/66 that were moving in the same direction. The Fusilier Battalion of the 26th was already approaching that objective.

Southern opening of the *Tiefenlinie* D
(Taken looking north from the Sunken Meadow E)

Masloved

Swiepwald
Southern point of the central sector B where it meets the sunken meadow E
(Taken looking towards the northeastern border of the sunken meadow)

As mentioned above, part of the slope was held by the 3rd Battalion IR 12, however the 3rd Company Pr. I/66 broke their resistance and captured the ridge, driving the retreating [Austrians] before them. The other two companies (2nd and 4th Pr. I/66) encountered little resistance and reached the crest at the same time as the 3rd Company. Along with the three companies mentioned above, the Fusilier Battalion of the 26th also arrived on the ridge. During its [earlier] advance towards the northern edge of the Swiepwald, it came under brisk fire from a small, mixed bag of Austrians, who soon fell back towards Másloved, pursueded by the Fusilier Battalion of the Pr. 26 as far as the eastern edge of the woods.

Meanwhile, in the face of combined, superior [enemy] forces (the 2nd, 3rd, 4th, 9th, 11th and 12th Companies of Pr. 66 and the Fusilier Battalion of the 26th) the Austrians on the ridge (the 3rd Battalion IR 26 and 3rd Battalion IR 12) were forced to abandon the position they had held with such courage, persistence and tenacity. Thereupon it was occupied by three combined Prussian companies (3rd, 2nd, and 4th Companies Pr. I/66), who then advanced to the southern border of that part of the wood designated T. The 2nd and 4th Companies deployed in skirmish lines along its eastern edge, while the 3rd Company occupied the south. The Fusilier Battalion of the 26th also went into position on the southern edge [of T] between that company (3rd Pr. I/66) and the 9th Company Pr. F/66, under *Premier Lieutenant* Gneist, which was further to the right (southwest).

For a long time, the 8th division of the Austrian IR III/12 resisted the advance of superior Prussian forces with well-aimed fire, only abandoning the sunken road when they were threatened with being outflanked and cut off. Before that they launched a strong counterattack in the face of such overwhelming odds that it had no chance of success. The Austrian 3rd Battalion IR 12 then retired south to the sunken road that ran from Másloved to Cistōves. In so doing they had to cross completely open ground and consequently suffered heavy losses from the Prussian rapid fire that pursued them. The 8th division [IR 12] took up their position at the sunken road in extended line and succeeded (with considerable support from friendly batteries) in preventing the enemy from breaking out of the woods, thereby covering the [remainder] of the battalion's retreat behind Másloved. When the division later learned that fresh Austrian troops had occupied the Másloved Hill, it withdrew to the brigade's assembly point.

Along with the Austrian 3rd Battalion IR 12, the 2nd and 3rd Battalions of IR 26 fighting alongside it were also forced out of the woods. The 1st Battalion IR 26 which had been covering several batteries of the 2nd Corps Artillery Reserve, arrived [in the Brigade area] at about 12:00 noon. In the fighting described above, the 3rd Battalion IR 12 lost Lieutenant Waicz killed, Captain Gayer and *Oberlieutenants* Dhonel and John seriously wounded, and Lieutenants Nitsch and Horný slightly wounded. *Oberlieutenants* Lenartovi and Suzdelevi were captured by the enemy. The Austrian IR 26 lost Captain Zuna and Lieutenant Biasi killed, and Major Barisani, Captain Perelli, Lieutenants Klar, Bitteri and Hartmann wounded. The Prussian formations facing them also suffered significant losses. The Fusilier Battalion of the Prussian 26th lost six officers within a short time of each other, the battalion commander (Major Schönholz) and three other officers were severely wounded, and *Premier Lieutenant* Ewald and Second Lieutenant Müller II were both killed.

At nearly the same time as 4th Corps, three brigades and the artillery reserve of the Austrian 2nd Corps moved out of their bivouac south of the Trotinka stream (between Trotina and Lochenic) and proceeded toward the Horenoves Hill R on the right of 4th Corps. The 2nd

Feldjäger Battalion (commanded by Major Lang Edel von Waldthurm) of Brigade Thom received the following orders at about 7:00 a.m.:

> At the same time Brigade Battery (Lobkovitz) goes into position on the hill south of Horenoves [Hill R], the battalion is to expedite its advance to that location, and to cover that position by occupying the ground to the west, on the far side of the pheasantry [*Fasanerie*] and to resist enemy encroachment in that area by all possible means. The brigade will follow on shortly.

Detaching one company of the 3rd division as an advance-guard (which in turn, detached two platoons to cover the right flank on the hills by Horenoves), the battalion immediately moved out via Sendrazic. The brigade battery separated from the battalion at the northwestern exit from Sendrazic and trotted off to the *Tummelplatz* (Hill R),[6] where it soon went into action.

The *Feldjäger* Battalion went into position with front facing west as follows: the 3rd division (Captain Zverina) on the right (covered to the north by the two platoons that had been sent forward to Horenoves), and the 2nd division (Captain *Graf* Cerini) on the left. The 1st division (Captain Mudroch) followed on behind the left flank as reserve. Even during the approach, the battalion (especially its more exposed left flank) suffered losses from enemy fire coming from the Havranec A and the central wooded sector B. Accordingly, it passed the pheasantry and moved into position as quickly as possible. Due to the difficult terrain [and probably the rapidity of its advance] the two divisions became somewhat separated so the 1st division was inserted in the developing gap. The 2nd division took up position on Hill Q, the 3rd about 400 paces west of the Horenoves dairy farm. The 1st division occupied an orchard and gullies north of Hill Q.

Shortly before 9:00 a.m. firing commenced against the Havranec and the central wooded sector. In the meantime, Colonel Thom reached the scene of the fighting with the four battalions of his brigade that were still available. The 1st division IR I/40 occupied the Horenoves dairy farm (in order to secure the right flank) and established contact on its right with the 27th *Feldjäger* Battalion [Brigade Brandenstein 4th Corps]. The main body of the brigade, with the 2nd and 3rd divisions of IR I/40 *Baron Rossbach* and the 2nd Battalion IR 40 in the first wave and the 2nd and 3rd Battalions IR 69 *Count Jellačić* in the second wave, took up position to the east of the pheasantry. The 1st Battalion IR 69 held the wooded slope between Sendrazic and Racic. The 3rd Battalion IR 40 was detached to the corps ammunition train. Brigade Henriquez remained on the Elbe at Trotina. The corps artillery reserve proceeded to the *Tummelplatz*, going into action beside Brigade Battery Thom, with front facing west. It fired on the Swiepwald and on the columns of the Prussian 7th Division.

At approximately 9:51 a.m. (according to the history of the Prussian 66th Infantry Regiment), following the withdrawal of one platoon of the 1st Company and the 2nd, 3rd, 4th, 11th, and 12th Companies of Pr. 66, only two Prussian platoons from the 1st Company along with stragglers from the remaining companies of the 66th and the Fusilier Battalion of the 67th, remained in the hotly contested central wooded sector B. The 2nd Battalion Pr. 66 was still

---

6   Ed. Note – On the map Hill 317 is located about 1,000 metres southeast of Horenoves. Originally indicated on the map with a little cross and the famous pair of Linden trees, I have identified it with the letter R. It was a conspicuous landmark and played an important role in the course of the battle.

being held in reserve in the sunken meadow E, however due to the detachment of the 6th Company to Hnevcoves, the battalion was only three companies strong. Of these, the rifle platoon [*Schützenzug*[7]] of the 8th Company (under Lieutenant Engholm) and its 8th Platoon (under Lieutenant Rieben) were deployed in the projection of the woods M facing Másloved and in the sunken road running along its northwestern edge.

These two platoons started a firefight with the Austrians who were already in the sunken road but suffered greatly from their returning fire. Those parts of the 1st Battalion Pr. 66, which had held the [eastern] border of the woods projecting towards Másloved, along with the Fusilier Battalion of Pr. 26, seemed to be under heavy pressure, for it was clear that the firing line was wavering and that numerous wounded were making their way to the rear.

After the Austrian battalions (2nd and 3rd Battalions IR 26 and the 3rd Battalion IR 12) had been forced out by the Prussian 2nd, 3rd, and 4th Companies Pr. I/66 and the Fusilier Battalion of Pr. 26, the Prussian companies appeared at the eastern border of the woods where they came under murderous artillery and rifle fire. Their repeated attempts to advance from the border of the woods were bloodily repelled. In the meantime, the Austrian 2nd Battalion IR 12 went into action. Supported by the 1st Battalion, it advanced [from behind Hill Q] to attack the Swiepwald. Even before the start of this attack (shortly before 9:30 a.m.) the Prussian 2nd Battalion Pr. 66, which was waiting in reserve in the sunken meadow E, received orders to occupy Hill S east of the sunken meadow. That was nearly the same spot where a little earlier the companies of the 1st Battalion Pr. 66 had been engaged. The attacking Austrians of the 1st and 2nd Battalions IR 12 thus came up against the Prussian 2nd Battalion Pr. 66, as well as fresh troops that were in the wooded projection M. The 6th division IR II/12 (together with the 1st Battalion) advanced across the open ground north of the track that ran from Másloved to the northern sector of the woods, while the 5th division IR II/12 advanced south of the above track. The 4th division IR II/12 was kept in reserve.

The Prussian 2nd Battalion Pr. 66 (only seven platoons strong) advanced under fire from the skirmish line of the 6th division IR II/12 to the edge of Hill S. Here it was spotted by the main body of the 6th division that was advancing in Divisionsmasse, and from which it received volley fire that forced it to retreat. Thereupon the 6th division (reinforced by the 4th division) attempted to launch an attack on the woods, but this (as well as another launched by the 4th division alone) collapsed in the face of the enemy's rapid fire (the enemy, meanwhile, had extended their line northwards as far as the southeast corner of the Havranec).

Despite this, groups of Austrian *Feldjäger* (presumably from the 27th and 2nd Battalions) that had managed to enter the Havranec fired into the left flank of the Prussian battalion. In response to this, the 7th Company Pr. II/66 (Captain Sobbe) swung towards the Havranec and dispatched a half platoon in that direction. The 5th Company Pr. II/66 (First Lieutenant Sallwürk) was also brought forward to check a column advancing from [the east], probably some of the 1st Battalion IR/12.

The 5th division IR II/12, which as mentioned above had advanced south of the road leading from Másloved to the northern sector of the woods, must have launched its attack

---

7   Tr. Note – In a Prussian company formed of two three-ranked platoons, the rear rank of each platoon included the best marksmen, who when the company column formed for battle, separated from their original platoons to form a third two-ranked platoon or '*Schützenzug*' which provided skirmishers, leaving the parent platoons with only two ranks.

on M at the same time as the Prussian Fusiliers of the 26th IR launched theirs towards Másloved. The skirmishers of the 9th, 11th, and 12th Companies Pr. F/26 hurried over the open ground towards the northwestern entrance to Másloved, followed by their *Soutien*[8] and the 10th Company Pr. F/ 26 that was in the second wave. The advance, however, was bloodily repelled by the Austrian batteries and the shattered Prussian Fusiliers had to fall back to the woods. At this point, according to Prussian sources, an Austrian infantry battalion appeared at the western edge of Másloved (presumably the 5th division IR II/12) and opened heavy fire on the retreating Prussians. The latter passed through the lines of their own 66th particularly its 3rd Company, which had supported the attack to the best of its ability. These Prussian companies were now able to bring the Austrian column to a standstill, but they could not prevent individual groups of Austrians from slipping into the woods. However, threatened by the 11th and 12th Companies Pr. F/66, which had advanced to the middle of the slope O, and after an intense hand-to-hand struggle, the Austrians were finally ejected. The Fusilier Companies of Pr. 66 then joined Captain Przychowski and again advanced with the Fusilier Battalion of the 26th. This rash advance cost the Fusilier Battalion over 100 men, including three officers wounded.

As all this was taking place, the Austrian *20th Feldjäger* Battalion of Brigade Württemberg came to the assistance of the hard-pressed troops of Brigade Brandenstein, but they were too late as the battalions of that brigade had already been forced out of the woods. With the repulse of the 5th division, it appeared that the gallant attacks of the 1st and 2nd Battalions IR 12 had come to an end. The two battalions now settled down to a firefight with the enemy, thereby preventing him from breaking out of the northern wooded sector towards Másloved. They held on in this position until they were relieved by troops of the 2nd Corps. The two above-mentioned battalions suffered numerous casualties. Captain Ljubojensky and Lieutenant Komárek were killed, and *Oberlieutenant* Vötter was mortally wounded and died in Lochenic. Lieutenants Seidl and Seifert were severely wounded, and Captain Wavrouš, commander of the 6th division, was lightly wounded.

The Prussians in the woods that projected toward Másloved M now found themselves in a very difficult situation; however, the 2nd Battalion Pr. 26 arrived at this point. As it advanced through the forest, heavy fire could be heard coming from the direction of its Fusilier Battalion. Accordingly, the commander of the 13th Infantry Brigade [General Major von Schwarzhoff] ordered it to swing towards Másloved and support the Fusiliers. However, because of the dense undergrowth, the battalion could only work its way forward slowly, eventually deploying at the edge of the woods on the right flank of its Fusilier Battalion. The 5th Company took up position in the corner of the woods T that projected toward the southeast (where the memorial to the

---

8   Tr. Note – After the *Schutzenzüge*, or rifle platoons, had been separated from the other platoons of the company and deployed, a portion (of the *Schützenzug*) were employed as skirmishers, the remainder as their supports or *Soutien*. As the *Exercise Manual for Infantry* describes in Section 40. 'Behind every skirmish line there must be a closed-up body of troops that can rapidly support [the skirmish line] but that is held back at a distance sufficient to avoid enemy rifle fire, about 150 paces on the exercise ground. This troop consists of the undeployed elements of the platoons employed to form the skirmish line, and conforms to the movements of the skirmish line providing immediate help and protection.' (Anon., *Exerzir-Reglement für die Infanterie der Königlich Preußischen Armee vom 25. Februar 1847. Neuabdruck under Berücksichtigung der bis zum 3. August 1870 ergangenen Abänderungen* (Berlin: 1870))

Austrian 13th *Feldjäger* Battalion now stands) with part of its front facing Másloved [east] and the other facing Lipa [south].

The Prussian battalion initially engaged in an extremely costly firefight with the Austrian 20th *Feldjägers* of Brigade Württemberg (2nd Corps). That brigade had first been ordered to proceed to Horenoves Hill R and deploy on the left beside Brigade Thom. However, upon its arrival it was ordered to take up a new position farther south and advance in the low ground between Másloved and Horenoves so as to support Brigade Brandenstein (which was already engaged). The brigade then formed up between Másloved and the pheasantry south of Horenoves with IR 57 *Archduke Mecklenburg-Schwerin* in the first wave, IR 47 *Baron Hartung* in the second and the 20th *Feldjägers* occupying Másloved on the left. The brigade battery was positioned on the Horenoves Hill for the time being.

When the 20th *Feldjägers* arrived in Másloved, *Herzog* von Württemberg [the Brigade Commander] realised that the Prussians intended to capture [the village]. In order to prevent this, and also to disengage those elements of Brigade Brandenstein that were still in action, the 20th *Feldjägers* were pushed forwards from the village toward the woods while occupation of the village was turned over to the 1st and 2nd Battalions, IR 47. The *Feldjägers* went into position with the 1st division to the west of Másloved, while the two other divisions deployed further to the north. The 2nd Company of the 1st division deployed as skirmishers at the western end of the village so that its right flank was in contact with IR 47, while its left rested on Rocket Battery Nr. 11/ IV. The 1st Company was initially in close order behind the skirmish line, and both fired on the enemy 400 paces distant, with good effect. As the Austrian forces to the left of the rocket battery changed position, however, the left flank of the company became exposed. Accordingly, Captain Klinzer extended the line with part of the 1st Company and employed the remainder in strengthening the skirmish line.

From the 2nd division, the 3rd Company went into position near the northern boundary of the village, while the 4th Company (Captain Genotte) advanced to the right to fire into the Prussian left flank. The latter company made it to within 150 paces of the edge of the woods, from where it opened an intense fire. It appeared to be having some effect since the enemy fire decreased, thereby providing the opportunity for a bayonet attack. This was repelled, however, with heavy losses, and the company had to fall back to its former position (*Oberlieutenant* Grubich was mortally wounded in that action). The Prussians then counterattacked in an attempt to force the *Feldjägers* from their position, but effective Austrian fire forced them back into the woods.

The Austrian *Feldjäger* company took advantage of that moment to launch a second assault. This time it made it to within 100 paces of the enemy before going to ground and for a long time maintaining heavy fire. However, seriously depleted by the Prussian rapid fire and in order to avoid being entirely wiped out, it fell back towards Másloved where it rejoined the 3rd Company. The 3rd division, commanded by Captain Urschitz, went into position about 300 paces north of Másloved. There it received orders from the Brigadier to attack the enemy forces in the woods. Sprinting across the 600-metre interval, it reached the enemy in a state of total exhaustion and deployed in line behind a bank at the edge of the field. Because [of the problems associated with getting over the bank] and in order to be able to attack the woods under more favourable conditions, it was decided to change position. At this critical moment the Prussians launched a counterattack against the division's front and flank; it was here that Lieutenants *Baron* Schmidburg and Führig fell, and Captain Urschitz and Lieutenants Hell and Dietrich were wounded. The division then rallied on the left flank of the 1st division, and along with the other two divisions, kept up a suppressing fire against the edge of the woods. Regarding this attack, the Prussians reported:

> The commander of the 2nd Battalion Pr. 26, Major Gilsa, observed the advance of the Austrian 20th *Feldjäger* Battalion from Másloved towards the woods, whereupon he immediately had the 7th Company advance from the woods and fire into the flank of the *Feldjäger*. With extreme precision, the two companies of the *Feldjäger* Battalion changed front (to face left) and attempted to return the Prussian fire, however in the meantime, the 6th and 8th Companies of the Prussian battalion also emerged from the woods and delivered a devastating *schnellfeuer*. The two *Feldjäger* companies (along with two other companies of their battalion that had hastened to their support) could no longer hold their position and had to fall back. Much of the Prussian 66th Infantry Regiment also took part in the fight against the Austrian *Feldjäger*.

In order to escape from the devastating fire of the Austrian artillery, however, the three Prussian companies mentioned above (the 6th, 7th, and 8th Companies Pr. II/26) were immediately forced to flee [back into the woods], while at the same time the last remnants of the 20th *Feldjägers* began their retreat towards Másloved. In this attack, Major Gilsa was shot in the back and two lieutenants were lightly wounded, along with greater losses among the men.

During this action (of Pr. II/26), the Fusilier Battalion of the [same regiment] fell back from the edge of the wooded area M to rally. The 11th and 12th Companies were [then] ordered by the regimental commander to resume their former position on the left wing. The 2nd Battalion (which had fallen back to the cleared slope O) had barely begun to reorganise when strong Austrian forces were spotted north of Másloved. Thereupon the battalion again advanced to the border of the wooded projection M (which, after the withdrawal of the Fusilier Battalion of Pr. 26, was only lightly held by elements of Pr. I/66).

As the Austrian 2nd and 3rd Battalions IR 26 renewed their assault on the woods, they were joined in their attack by the 13th *Feldjägers*. These belonged to Major General Fleischhacker's Brigade of the Austrian 4th Corps, which had left its bivouac at Nedelist and set out on the road toward Másloved at 8:00 a.m. The 13th *Feldjägers* formed the head of the column, followed (by order of the corps commander) by the entire corps artillery reserve, then the two infantry regiments and finally the brigade battery (the latter could not move forward because the corps artillery reserve was in front of it).

South of Másloved, the 13th *Feldjägers* were directed by Major General Fleischhacker towards the southeastern corner of the Swiepwald T to prevent the enemy from debouching from the woods. Even as the battalion deployed from column of march into battle formation, a Prussian shell burst in the middle of the 1st Platoon of the 2nd Company, wounding several *Jägers* (the air pressure of its flight also rendered *Oberlieutenant* Sturm incapable of combat). At about 9:15 a.m., the battalion reached the eastern end of the southern slope N and found the border of the tall woods on the western half of Hill K, as well as the cleared slope in front of them N, already held by the enemy.

The 9th Company Pr. F/66 and a platoon from the 11th Company Pr. F/66 were on the slope itself. The 5th Company Pr. II/27 had its right flank resting on the junction of the Benátek–Cistōves–Másloved road (where, along with other monuments, is the memorial to *Oberst Brigadier* Poeckh). On its left (to the northeast) it was in contact with the 8th Company Pr.

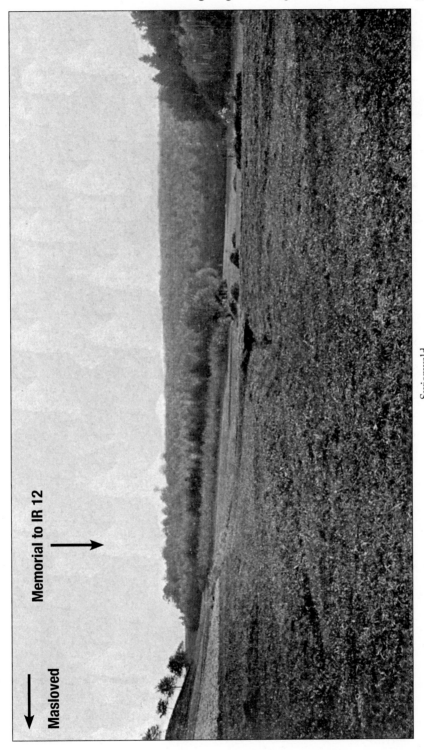

Swiepwald

The sunken meadow E bounded to the south and west by woods, open to the east [note the height and steepness of the embankment]

Swiepwald

Eastern end of the southern slope as far as the gullies. Battleground of the Austrian 13th *Feldjäger* Battalion, then the right wing of Brigade Poeckh, and finally, the left wing of Brigade Saffran. Photographed looking south from the road along the ridge [F – F]

II/27, which was positioned at the foot of Hill K. The 8th Company Pr. II/27 was in contact on the left with the 10th Company Pr. F/27, which was positioned at the edge of the tall timber. Adjoining the latter was the 12th Company Pr. F/27, and behind them both, the 11th Company Pr. F/27 with front facing southeast. These five companies fought against what was left of the three battalions of Brigade Appiano that had been engaged there as well as against [those parts of Brigade Brandenstein that had ventured this far]. The other seven companies of Pr. 27 were similarly engaged with those parts of Brigade Appiano that were in the process of retreating.

The Austrian 13th *Feldjägers* deployed the 1st and 2nd Companies (under the command of Captain Henn) in a skirmish line and established itself firmly in the new growth on the eastern slope T, while the other four companies (the 2nd and 3rd divisions) remained closed-up in reserve about 100 paces behind. The enemy was about 300–400 paces away (they had found excellent cover behind the checkerboard of piled cordwood that was arranged on the cleared slope N) and their *schnellfeuer* at this range against the *Feldjäger* (who were at a lower elevation) was devastating. The *Feldjäger* were not slow to reply however, and their calm, well-aimed shooting exacted a heavy toll from the Prussians, despite their excellent cover. The firefight continued in this fashion until the *Feldjägers* realised that the Prussians facing them were being reinforced (presumably by elements of Pr. 26 and Pr. 67). Accordingly, the battalion commander (Captain Poschacher) had the 3rd and 4th Companies deploy as skirmishers, the former extending the right flank of the skirmish line, the latter the left. Soon afterwards, Captain Poschacher was severely wounded in the face by a rifle shot. Later his replacement Captain Strachovsky, was himself mortally wounded in the abdomen by shrapnel. Command of the battalion then passed to Captain Wenz. Regardless of all this, the brave *Feldjäger* maintained their position on the eastern slope T, repelling repeated Prussian attacks and eventually forcing the enemy to abandon their position. If the *Feldjägers* had now received prompt and determined support, their courageous action would doubtlessly have led to great success.

According to the Prussian accounts, the three Fusilier companies (the 10th, 11th, and 12th) of Pr. F/27 that were engaged in heavy fighting with parts of Brigade Brandenstein and the 13th *Feldjäger* Battalion at the edge of the tall timber were under pressure from three sides. Their losses mounted, especially among 10th Company, which lost all its officers. The company commander, Captain von Westerhagen, was hit by a rifle bullet in the abdomen, and Lieutenant von Byern was also shot. Both wounds proved fatal. Lieutenants von Steophasius and Pever received minor wounds. The 11th Company (Captain *Graf* Finkenstein) was still in close order when it too came under extremely heavy fire, not only from the front, but also from the right flank where the 13th *Feldjägers* had established themselves in a small gully nearly in the rear of the 10th Company. Shortly thereafter, the *Feldjäger* slipped between the 10th and 12th Companies, rendering the situation even more critical and requiring drastic measures.

Accordingly, *Premier Lieutenant* Helmuth was sent forward with a platoon (the 6th). He made his way through the thick undergrowth and reached the border of the woods at its south-eastern corner. Captain Finkenstein followed Helmuth's platoon with the other two platoons. Without realising it, they passed between the combatants and arrived at the southeastern edge of the woods (not far from Helmuth's platoon) practically unscathed. From there Captain *Graf* Finkenstein spotted an Austrian battery towards which he immediately advanced with his company. However, they had only covered a short stretch when Captain Finkenstein fell without a sound, struck in the temple by a shell fragment, and the company poured back into the woods. Things were no better for the 12th Company, which could only defend itself with extreme difficulty.

The companies of the 2nd Battalion Pr. 27 (especially the 5th and 8th Companies that were in the front line) also suffered heavy casualties and lost their cohesion. The 8th Company, attacked simultaneously from front and flank, was heavily engaged. Accordingly, these two companies were to be reinforced by the 6th and 7th Companies Pr. II/27 that were stationed to their rear. The former lost its way however, ended up going in a southeasterly direction and then came under fire from the left. This was extremely remarkable since (aside from the 7th Company) the only troops known to be in the vicinity were [Prussian] Fusiliers. It was therefore assumed that the company was taking friendly fire, but it soon transpired that it was facing Austrian *Feldjäger* (presumably from the 13th *Feldjäger* Battalion), who were adept at infiltrating between the gaps in the Prussian lines, concealing themselves and then, when the opportunity presented itself, opening fire with great accuracy.

The [6th Company Pr. II/27] had resumed its advance (after establishing contact with the 7th Company and driving off the Austrian *Jäger*) when it suddenly came under fire again, but this time from the right. Accordingly, a platoon (the 4th), under *Premier Lieutenant* Haack, had to be deployed as skirmishers to secure that flank. Laboriously making their way forward (and at times clearing their front of the ubiquitous Austrian *Jäger*), the two companies reached the edge of the woods (west of the southeastern tip, close beside the 11th Fusilier Company Pr. 27), where the rifle platoons found cover, some behind the stacks of cordwood, some behind trees, others out in the meadow behind haystacks. *Premier Lieutenant* Haack and his platoon (4th Platoon, 6th Company) reached the border of the woods farther to the west and, after a short firefight, pushed forward and established themselves in the deeply sunken Másloved–Cistōves road. The 5th and 8th Companies followed the 6th and 7th through the woods, and even though the latter had previously passed over the same ground, came under fire from Austrian *Feldjäger* that were concealed everywhere. *Portepee Fähnrich* [officer candidate entitled to wear a sword knot] Hellmuth was killed during the advance. Both companies [the 5th and 8th] reached the southern border where the Benátek–Cistōves road leaves the forest. The 8th Company took up position to its east (where the memorial to the Austrian 8th *Feldjäger* now stands), the 5th Company to its west (behind the 9th Company).

Let us now repeat our earlier description of the positions of the 1st Battalion Pr. 27 and the 9th Company Pr. F/27. Lieutenant Hanstein and his platoon (7th Platoon, 4th Company) were established in the meadow north of Cistōves behind a rise in the ground, while farther to the east Lieutenant von Schroeder, with the 5th Rifle Platoon, had emerged from the southern boundary of the woods. The 9th Company Pr. F/27 was at the southeastern tip of the woods, and the 4th Company Pr. I/27 several hundred paces to its east inside the woods. The 2nd and 3rd Companies were behind the 1st and 4th Companies. At that time (about 9:45 a.m.) Cistōves was only held by a few groups of skirmishers left behind by the Austrian 4th *Feldjäger* Battalion and IR 62 [Brigade Appiano]. The weak fire that Lieutenant Hanstein's platoon received made it evident that it was only lightly defended. Accordingly, he charged into the western part of the village and was able to capture it without significant losses. Somewhat later than Hanstein, Schroeder's rifle platoon also advanced into Cistōves, this time entering it from the east, and without knowledge of each other's presence, the two platoons then fought their way forward to the southern edge of the village. Here Hanstein (having observed elements of the Austrian IR 62 withdrawing to Lipa in close order) advanced out of the village and fired on them. As the two Prussian platoons met, they saw that an Austrian column was advancing from the south towards the village, and that a second was advancing to the east of the first column towards the forest. This was the Austrian Brigade of Major General Fleischhacker, whose attack will be described below.

From his position in the woods, the commander of the 9th Company Pr. F/27 (Captain Buddenbruck) observed the advance of Hanstein's and Schroeder's platoons toward Cistōves and resolved to support them if needed. When he appeared [with his company] at the southern border of the woods, however, both platoons had already vanished from sight. Meanwhile, Austrian shells from Chlum and Lipa were falling on the edge of the woods with uncanny accuracy, so he quickly led his company over the meadow onto the rising ground that culminated in a hillock directly northwest of Cistōves (where the memorial to the Prussian 27th Infantry Regiment now stands).

While the 11th Company Pr. F/27 (*Graf* Finkenstein), as well as the companies of the 2nd Battalion Pr. 27, were being forced out of their position in the centre of the woods by the splendid actions of the Austrian 13th *Feldjäger* Battalion, the 1st Battalion Pr. 26 appeared at that location. It had entered the woods at the re-entrant angle on the northern edge and made it past an abatis blocking the road to Másloved. Further advance into the woods proved extremely difficult due to the dense undergrowth.

Near Hill K in the centre of the woods, the riflemen of the 1st Company suddenly came under heavy flanking fire from 200–300 stragglers of Brigades Brandenstein and Appiano. These had fallen back from the northern and western parts of the woods (after the 9th Company Pr. F/27 had retreated there to regroup) and occupied the knoll. Fighting without organisation or any sort of overall command, these stragglers were unable to hold their own against the Prussian skirmishers and had to fall back to the southwest.

Southeast of Hill K was a saddle where the 1st Battalion Pr. 26 and an element of the Austrian IR 12 met, and towards which the 2nd and 4th Companies turned. These were able, with significant losses, to repel the Austrian force. In the meantime, the 1st and 3rd Companies Pr. I/26 moved onto Hill K where they provided an outstanding target for the Austrian batteries at Chlum. For that reason, the battalion commander (Major Paucke) decided to leave only the 1st Company on the knoll while he advanced with the three other companies to the southern edge of the woods. However, this was already held by elements of Pr. 27, so he moved his men into the gap between the 6th and 7th Companies Pr. II/27, which had recently come down from the hill. This was at the very moment when Brigade Fleischhacker advanced to attack the southern boundary of the woods after capturing the village of Cistōves.

The 1st Company Pr. I/26 which had remained on the knoll soon caught the attention of some of the Austrian 13th *Feldjäger* Battalion, who took them in the flank and threw them off. However, the Prussians did not fall back very far, and when they realised the *Feldjäger's* limited numbers, advanced and recaptured the knoll. The *Feldjäger* fell back to the west where they ran into the advancing 2nd Battalion Pr. 67 and were dispersed. Some of them made their way to the northern and western border of the woods, everywhere taking advantage of the situation and making skilful use of the terrain (the Prussian reports also bear witness to their outstanding fieldcraft). Thanks to the steadfast endurance of this battalion, the other three brigades of 4th Corps and a part of the artillery reserve were able to deploy for action without interference.

The [main body] of the 13th *Feldjäger* held its original position in the young growth T, its right flank threatened by the advance of the 1st Battalion Pr. 67th and its rear by the 5th Company

Pr. II/26. During the attack of the first wave of Brigade Poeckh (which moved forward through 13th *Jäger*'s position) the right flank of the *Feldjäger* Battalion joined in the advance. It was only when this attack miscarried (thereby making the position of the battalion untenable) did they withdraw from the woods. Five companies went back to Másloved and took up a position covering the batteries of 4th Corps that were west of the village. The 4th Company (Captain Veith) shifted southwards and linked up with the brigade at Cistōves.

The Austrian General Staff work says the following about the phases of the battle outlined above: 'The confusion of this bitter forest fighting was extreme. The Prussian battalions were every bit as scattered as the Austrian. Large elements of both sides had either bypassed or passed through each other and were fighting while thoroughly mixed up.' During this fighting Lieutenant General von Fransecky arrived on the right flank of the 1st Battalion Pr. 26. Since his horse had been shot from under him, he proceeded on foot, and to gain a better picture of the situation made his way to Hill K, where (from the edge of the tall timber) he hoped to be able to see the progress of the fighting in the cleared areas to the east and southeast. Suddenly a small detachment of the Austrian 13th *Feldjäger* Battalion burst out of the tall timber, drove off the Prussian riflemen that were there and surrounded the General, who after gathering a few stragglers, drew his sword and prepared to defend himself. After a brief hand-to-hand fight, the men of the Prussian 26th and 66th infantry regiments that had hastened to the spot overwhelmed the few Austrian *Feldjäger* and freed the Divisional Commander from his critical situation.

Soon after the Prussian 27th had entered the woods, the commander of the 14th [Prussian] Infantry Brigade (General von Gordon) became convinced that the 7th Division was too weak to hold its ground successfully. When he observed Brigade Fleischhacker advancing toward Cistōves at about 9:45 a.m. (with the main body of the Division already engaged) he ordered the two Musketeer Battalions of the 67th (which constituted the Divisional reserve) to advance to the support of the hard-pressed 27th. The two Musketeer Battalions in questions were originally intended to remain in the village of Cerekvic, which until this point had formed a strong defensive position for the advance-guard of the 7th Division. They were to hold it as a strongpoint and organise it for defence. However, the battalions had hardly begun to carry out the requisite measures when they received orders to follow the main body of the Division to Benátek. It must have been about 8:00 a.m. when the two battalions (which lacked their full complement) moved out from Cerekvic. The 1st and 8th Companies consisted of only two platoons each since one platoon had been detached from each and assigned to the Divisional artillery to provide cover for the guns. The 5th Company was entirely absent because it was guarding the supply train in Vostrom.

At about 8:30 a.m. the battalions reached Benátek, where they were initially positioned to the north of the village in a meadow (beside the main body of the Division that was waiting in readiness). From this latter, the Fusilier Battalion and the 1st Battalion Pr. 66 were sent forward to support the advance-guard; soon afterwards (at about 8:45 a.m.) the remaining four battalions were ordered into action. According to the history of the Prussian 67th Infantry Regiment it was not long before the reserve was also ordered to advance. This could not have been before 9:30 a.m. The two battalions passed the village of Benátek (under extremely heavy shellfire) and followed the road toward Cistōves. Since the fight seemed to be raging most heavily on the extreme right wing, the commander of the 67th, Colonel von Bothmer, ordered the 1st Company (which as noted above consisted of only two platoons) to precede the 2nd Battalion as an advance-guard. The latter (with only eight platoons) under Major von Zedwitz followed the company as support.

The 1st Battalion (consisting of three companies) under Lieutenant Colonel Hochstetter swung somewhat to the left before entering the woods and moved to the left of the battle line (that is, to the southeast). The 2nd Company was in the lead followed to the left rear by the 3rd and 4th Companies. When the 2nd Company (with the skirmishing platoon deployed ahead) had got as far as the road from Másloved, it suddenly came under fire from Austrian skirmishers posted to its left behind the piles of cordwood. The company commander, Captain von Drigalski, deployed the skirmishing platoon (the 4th) to the left and drove off the Austrian skirmishers, who fell back through the northern cleared area O. This platoon then took up position south of the Másloved road (with front facing southeast), about 300 paces west of the hunting lodge that stood there. The 3rd and 4th Companies (each with a platoon of skirmishers thrown out ahead) soon met up with some of Pr. 26th and Pr. 66 that were in combat, whom they joined in suppressing the opposing Austrian skirmishers. Following them, they climbed the northern cleared area O under extremely heavy fire and took position (front facing southeast) some 50 paces north of where the road from Másloved entered the woods. As these two companies were climbing the hill (through the cleared area O), an Austrian *Feldjäger* Battalion approached the crest of the ridge from the southeast and would undoubtedly have surprised the two Prussian companies if Captain Drigalski [2nd Company], noticing the Austrian battalion, had not opened fire on its left flank at a range of 500 paces and forced it to fall back. According to Prussian sources, the Austrian battalion was supposed to have been the 13th *Feldjägers*, but in fact, it was only elements thereof. In the meantime, the two other platoons of the 2nd Company turned somewhat to the southwest and, crossing the Másloved road [F–F], reached the western end of the southern slope N, where they were brought to a halt by sudden, heavy fire from the Austrian 13th *Feldjäger* Battalion. As they sought cover behind the piles of cordwood, the two Prussian platoons kept up brisk fire on the Austrian *Jägers*, while the 3rd and 4th Companies were engaged in a hot fight with stragglers from Brigade Brandenstein that had established themselves in the sunken road that lay before them. The three Prussian companies remained engaged until the attack of the first wave of Brigade Poeckh. The 2nd Battalion Pr. 67 and the attached 1st Company Pr. I/67 were held up for a long time by the resistance of isolated groups of Austrians scattered through the woods. According to their regimental history (as well as that of the Prussian 27th Infantry Regiment), they first reached the southern boundary of the woods facing Cistōves just as Brigade Poeckh was entering the woods. According to the Austrian General Staff work (as well as the history of the Prussian 26th Infantry Regiment) this took place at 10:15 a.m., whereas the history of Pr. 27th asserts that the attack of Brigade Poeckh did not take place until 10:45 a.m.[9]

The advance of the 2nd Battalion and the 1st Company Pr. I/67 proceeded as follows. The 1st and 6th Companies (with the regimental commander, Colonel von Bothmer, in the lead) turned left off the Cistōves–Benátek road [W–W] before reaching the woods, then fighting constantly, reached the southern boundary where they immediately joined in the fighting of Pr. 27. Upon entering the forest, Captain Laue of the 1st Company had his left hand smashed by a shell fragment.

---

9   Author's note – This is not the only case in which the times given by individual regimental histories, both Austrian and Prussian, differ significantly from each other, as well as from the Austrian General Staff work

In the meantime, the 7th and 8th Companies advanced further on the Benátek–Cistōves road, but the ground was so slippery they made extremely slow progress. They had covered barely half the distance when a report arrived that the advance-guard (which was on the left) was in dire need of support. Therefore, they immediately left the road and reached the southern border of the woods in a few minutes. Proceeding further along the edge of the woods, they reached the position where the men of the 27th (facing the northern point of Cistōves) were under extremely heavy fire. At the same time, the 1st and 6th Companies were already in combat further east along the border of the woods. While this was taking place, the other three brigades of the Austrian 4th Corps entered the battle.

At about 9:30 a.m. a Prussian shell exploded near the Corps Commander, Lieutenant Field Marshall *Graf* Festetics, on the hill west of Másloved, tearing off the front of his left foot. His deputy [*Ad Latus*], Lieutenant Field Marshall Mollinary, assumed command of the corps.

The batteries of Brigade Poeckh and Archduke Josef joined the line of the corps artillery reserve west of Másloved. All in all, there were now eight gun batteries and one rocket battery: four south of the road running from Másloved into the woods (2/IV, 1/IV, 3/IV, 4/IV) and five north of the same road (7/IV, 8/IV, 5/IV, 9/IV, 10/IV) [these all appear to be gun batteries, the rocket battery numbered 11/IV is not mentioned]. Even while Brigade Brandenstein was fighting in the woods, 2nd Corps (as mentioned above), which had completed its concentration between Másloved and Horenoves, sent Brigade Württemberg forward to support them. Up to this point, the battle for possession of the Swiepwald was inconclusive. The last Prussian reserves had been ordered into the woods; it would now be continued by the Austrian side with fresh forces.

Let us summarise the course of the action up to this point. At about 8:00 a.m. four battalions of the Prussian advance-guard attacked the north and northwestern border of the Swiepwald, which at that time was only held by a half battalion of Austrians. The Austrian companies were forced back towards the centre of the woods. They were pursued by several Prussian companies that succeeded in establishing a firm foothold on the highest knoll in the woods K and on the ridgeline. The Prussians thereby gained a significant tactical advantage. The right wing of the Prussian advance-guard (two battalions strong) advanced through the northwestern part of the woods toward the south, where they came up against three battalions of the Austrian Brigade Appiano. They defeated these after a short, but extremely intense fight. One battalion of the latter departed to rejoin its brigade at Chlum, the two remaining battalions took up a new position in the sunken road, several groups fell back to Cistōves. Two Prussian [companies] then launched an attack on Cistōves (which was only held by a few Austrian stragglers) and drove the latter out of the village. On the Prussian left wing, a battalion took the central sector of the woods B. Reinforced by a second battalion, the two Prussian battalions engaged two battalions of the Austrian IR 12 that were advancing from the east. At 9:00 a.m. the main body of the Prussian 7th Division (and somewhat later, its reserve) attacked. Five out of a total of seven battalions (the Fusilier and 2nd Battalions Pr. 26, the 1st and 2nd Battalions Pr. 66, and the 1st Battalion Pr. 67) attacked toward the southeast, and two (the 1st Battalion Pr. 26 and the 2nd Battalion Pr. 67) toward the south.

The Prussian effort (which finally achieved success) was primarily directed at reaching the crest of the ridge that was defended by four battalions of Brigade Brandenstein. The Austrian battalions fell back toward Másloved, which was held by two battalions of Brigade Württemberg. The Austrian 20th *Feldjäger* Battalion took up position west of Másloved and continued an ongoing firefight with the Prussians. At about 9:40 a.m. nearly the entire Swiepwald was in Prussian hands and only the part T across from the southern cleared area was still stubbornly held by the Austrian 13th *Feldjägers*.

Despite repeated efforts, the Prussians were unable to break out of the woods. They were blocked in the southeast by the 13th *Feldjägers*, in the east by the 20th *Feldjägers*, and in the northeast by two battalions of IR 12. They were also held in check by the Austrian batteries that had gone into action west of Másloved. The southern margin of the woods and the knolls K and L were raked by fire from the Austrian batteries at Chlum. The situation of the Prussian battalions in the woods was extremely difficult, particularly due to the heavy Austrian artillery fire. However, since the Austrians seemed determined to capture the woods, new fighting flared up at about 10:00 a.m.

Section II

The attack of Brigades Fleischhacker and Poeckh as well as other events from 10:00 – 11:30 a.m.

By 10:00 a.m., the entire Prussian 7th Division was already committed to the Swiepwald as follows. On the left wing (north and northeast), in the central sector B as well as the Havranec A, was the Fusilier Battalion Pr. 67, the 2nd Battalion Pr. 66 (now rejoined by its 6th Company that had earlier been detached to Hnewcowes) and the 1st Company Pr. I/66. The 10th Company Pr. F/66 was located in the western wooded sector C.

The 2nd, 3rd, and 4th Companies Pr. I/66, as well as the 6th, 7th, and 8th Companies Pr. II/26 (behind which the Fusilier Battalion Pr. 26 rallied), were in the projection of the woods toward Másloved M. To the right of these (to the southwest), in the southern cleared area N, was the 9th Company Pr. F/66. The 3rd and 4th Companies Pr. 1/67 were located on the crest of Hill L north of the road, while south of the road was the 2nd Company Pr. I/67. On the northern cleared area O were the 11th and 12th Companies Pr. F/66.

In the projecting angle of the eastern border of the woods T south of the Másloved road (where the memorial to the Austrian 13th *Feldjäger* Battalion now stands) was the 5th Company Pr. II/ 26. On and near Hill K was 1st Battalion Pr. 26. At the southern border of the woods, the 11th, 7th, 6th, 8th, and 5th Companies Pr. 27 were located, the first three to the west of the southeastern point, the last two east and west of the road from Benátek to Cistőves [W–W]. The 9th Company Pr. F/27 was outside the woods on the hill northwest of Cistőves with its front facing east. At the southwestern point of the woods was the 1st Battalion Pr. 27. The 10th and 12th Companies Pr. F/27 were north of the track [F–F], just west of Hill K. The 1st, 6th, 7th and 8th Companies Pr. I–II/67 were advancing on the Benátek–Cistőves road [W–W].

The Hanstein and Schroeder platoons had already entered Cistőves, and soon afterwards the 4th Platoon of the 6th Company Pr. II/67 (under *Premier Lieutenant* Haack) established itself outside Cistőves in the ditch of the Másloved–Cistőves road. Aside from stragglers from Brigades Brandenstein and Appiano, the only forces of the Austrian 4th Corps that were still fighting in the Swiepwald were those of the 13th *Feldjäger* Battalion at the eastern end of the southern slope T, thereby covering the deployment of the other three brigades of the corps.

Brigade Archduke Josef deployed east of Másloved at 9:30 a.m. with Brigade Poeckh intending to form up to its left. However, Lieutenant Field Marshal Mollinary (who was now commanding the corps) ordered both brigades, as well as Brigade Fleischhacker, to shift westward. Brigade Fleischhacker (which was at the head of the corps) had received orders during its march to Másloved to change direction towards Cistőves and form up alongside and to the left of Brigade Brandenstein. The orders for Brigade Poeckh, which had just started to deploy, went as follows: 'It was to attack towards the Swiepwald, with its right wing brushing the southern end of Másloved, passing through the gaps between the batteries and between Brigades Brandenstein and Fleischhacker.' For Brigade Archduke Josef the orders read: 'It was to move out in the second wave of the corps, with its front along the sunken road that ran between Másloved–Chlum.'

Brigade Poeckh completed its concentration, and then moved out in *Divisionsmassen* through the gaps between the batteries on the high ground toward the southeastern side of the woods, with the 8th *Feldjäger* Battalion (on the left) and IR 51 (on the right) in the first wave, and IR 37 *Archduke Joseph* in the second wave [in reality the third wave, see below]. The brigade took up position along the Másloved–Lipá sunken road (with its right wing near the spot where it joined the Cistőves–Másloved sunken road) front facing northwest, about 500 paces from the southeastern point of the woods. The 2nd Battalion IR 21 *Reischach* and the 1st Battalion IR 32 *d'Este* closed up behind the left wing of the first wave. After their relief from outpost duty at Horenoves, they were supposed to rejoin their brigade, Brigade Wöber [formerly Brigade Kreyssern] of 8th Corps. In Sendrazic they came under rifle and cannon fire. Accordingly, they left the road and proceeded up the hill to their right, where they followed 4th Corps which was advancing past them. When investigations revealed that Brigade Wöber was no longer in Nedelišt, the two battalions made themselves available to the Brigadier, Colonel Poeckh, from whom they received orders to follow IR 51 as second wave in *Bataillons Massenlinie*. This took place at about 9:00 a.m.

As soon as space permitted, Brigade Archduke Josef also marched to the left and followed Brigade Poeckh, forming up behind the (in part) deeply sunken road that branches off from the west side of Másloved to Chlum. There the brigade was ordered to halt by the corps commander who designated it corps reserve. It deployed with front facing west, its orders read: 'The 30th *Feldjäger* Battalion (on the right) and IR 68 *Baron Steininger* (on the left) [will constitute] the first wave, and IR 67 *Ritter von Schmerling* the second wave. Brigade Battery Nr. 4/IV is to open fire alongside the corps artillery reserve.' Thus 4th Corps was in a position to launch an enveloping attack, however this did not happen. At that time assaults were generally undertaken battalion by battalion, which (as the Prussian reports emphasised), was particularly fortunate for them. Brigade Fleischhacker was the first to advance to the attack. It deployed in the low ground about 1,000 paces east of Cistőves, with IR 6 *Coronini* in the first wave, IR 61 *Archduke Thronfolger* in the second wave and the brigade battery on the left wing [as described earlier, the brigade's *Feldjäger* Battalion, the 13th, was already heavily committed in the woods].

Prior to the attack, the Austrian batteries at Chlum and Másloved brought the Swiepwald (wherever possible) under an even more intense barrage than before. After a few rounds from its own battery, Brigade Fleischhacker advanced. In accordance with Major General Fleischhacker's orders, the 1st Battalion IR 6 advanced against the southern border of the Swiepwald, while the 2nd and 3rd Battalions IR 6 advanced against Cistőves. The second wave (IR 61) was to follow behind and relieve the first wave. If things turned out badly, it would [cover the retreat or the first wave] and allow them to pass through its lines.

Of the battalions of IR 6, the 1st and 2nd formed up in *Bataillons Massen Linie*, the 3rd in *Divisions Massen Linie*. The advance ensued without preparation despite enemy flanking fire, which caused serious problems for the 1st Battalion on the right wing (the 1st Battalion marched with such precision, it was said, that it looked as if it was on the parade square).

During this advance (about 800 paces from Cistōves) Captain Fischer of the Corps General Staff brought orders from the Brigadier: 'For the time being the entire regiment is to head for Cistōves, the 1st Battalion IR 6 is to direct its advance toward the red house.'[1] In accordance with these orders, the 1st Battalion proceeded to the northeastern corner of Cistōves as far as the aforementioned house, where it received [new] orders from the regimental commander to attack the woods on the right, specifically that part in which the enemy had sought cover behind the cordwood, and from which the regiment had received flanking fire during its advance. At this point the village of Cistōves was held by two platoons of the Pr. 27. On the hill directly northwest of Cistōves was the 9th Company Pr. F/27 (Captain von Buddenbrock). According to Prussian accounts, there were no other [Prussian] troops in the vicinity. However, later events suggest that not only had the 11th Company Pr. F/27 advanced to the southern boundary of the wood (near the southeastern tip), but that the companies of the 2nd Battalion Pr. 27 were also near [the same location].

The commander of the 1st Battalion IR 6 (Captain von Findenigg) had the leading company (*Oberlieutenant* Schäfer) deploy as skirmishers while the battalion swung to the right, and then in *Bataillons Masse* charged the border of the woods. The battalion carried out all the evolutions described about 400 paces from the edge of the forest, all the while under continuous enemy fire. However, everything did not go to plan. The lead company (that had been deployed as skirmishers) drifted over to the left (towards the position held by the 9th Company Pr. F/27), thereby exposing the front of its own battalion to the full effect of the enemy's fire. This caused great confusion in the ranks of the attacking formation, which was so thoroughly disorganised that it became little more than a large mob. The main body made it to within 80 paces of the Prussians (with extremely heavy losses) but was unable to go any further due to the enemy's *schnellfeuer*. Accordingly, the advance came to a halt while the battalion sought cover in a small, inadequate, hollow. Shortly thereafter it retired to a fold in the ground some 200 paces to the rear re-group. It then fell back to Cistoves and finally took up position east of the village on the road to Másloved.

From there it was able (with great difficulty) to prevent the enemy from advancing against the right flank of the brigade. During the assault on the woods, the 1st Battalion IR 6 did not fire a shot. Only during the retreat did individual groups rally around Captain Nentwig and *Oberlieutenants* Brosch and Martini and open fire against the 9th Company Pr. F/27 that was outflanking them. Due to the [Prussian] *schnellfeuer* however, those groups [that had been rallied by *Oberlieutenants* Brosch and Martini] were forced to fall back to the sunken road on their right, from which they renewed their fire against the Prussian company.

While the 1st Battalion IR 6 was attacking the woods, the 2nd and 3rd Battalions IR 6, as well as the 5th and 6th divisions IR II/62, attacked the village of Cistoves. The latter two divisions (after their retreat from the Swiepwald) had taken up position on the Másloved–Lípa sunken road and later (at the request of Major General Fleischhacker) closed up to the left wing of his advancing brigade. According to the regimental history of IR 62, the 1st Battalion

---

1   Tr. Note – According to Ditfurth, Vol 2, p.66, the order read '*and thus the 1st Battalion is to direct its advance toward a widely visible red brick building*'.

took part in the capture of Cistoves and in the further fighting of Brigade Fleischhacker in and around the village. In the Austrian General Staff work however, there is no mention of this. According to that account, after its retreat from the Swiepwald to the Cistoves–Lípa sunken road (to the south of Cistoves) the battalion stopped there to rally. Our account of the fighting is based on the *regimental* history.

Of the forces attacking Cistoves, the 2nd Battalion IR 6 attacked the northern part of the village, the 3rd Battalion IR 6 and the 1st Battalion IR 62, as well as the 5th and 6th divisions IR II/62, attacked the south. The greater part of the two Prussian platoons of Pr. 27 under Lieutenants Hanstein and Schroeder were manning the southern perimeter of the village while the rest were on the east. These opened a devastating *schnellfeuer* on the attackers at short range, and the attackers did not reply with even a single shot. The Austrian 2nd Battalion IR 6 had to fall back, not only had it to face fire from the village but also from the woods. During the retreat the battalion commander (*Graf* Attems) was shot through the knee, whereupon Captain von Rácz assumed command. The 3rd Battalion IR 6 (under Captain Saric) had better luck. Advancing in *Divisionsmassen* it took advantage of some dead ground and escaped the flanking fire coming from the woods. This attack succeeded in capturing a number of farmsteads to the south, thereby gaining a foothold in the village. The regimental commander, Major Kornberger, then sent the 2nd Battalion IR 6 forward again, this time deploying two companies from the 3rd Battalion and three companies from the 2nd Battalion IR 6 as skirmishers. This dense skirmish line delivered throughout, a heavy fire nearly equal to that of the Prussians, after which they joined in the assault. The skirmish line, along with those in close order, drove the enemy back and forced their way into the village, linking up with the 1st Battalion IR 6 [that had earlier fallen back to the sunken road after its failed attack on the woods]. The 5th division IR II/62 (commanded by Major *Baron* Sterneck) advanced against the northern end of the village, and the 6th division against the south. During the advance, both divisions came under heavy fire from front and flank. It was here that Lieutenant Krecker-Drostmar died a hero's death.

The [1st and 2nd divisions] of the 1st Battalion IR 62 formed up in *Divisionsmassen*, while the 3rd division was held in reserve. Lieutenant Colonel *Baron* Appel, with the 1st and 2nd divisions, burst through the southern enclosure (which in part had to be pulled down by Pioneers) at a fast run and made it to the centre of the village where they ran into the retreating Prussians (who suffered significant losses in the brief hand-to-hand struggle that ensued). Both the Prussian officers, Hannstein and Schroeder, as well as a large number of unwounded men (47 according to Prussian sources) were captured. The rest of the Prussians made it to the western side of the village and from there out into open country (a few hid themselves in cellars and lofts where they remained until the arrival of the Prussian Guards Corps). The captured Prussians were escorted via Lípa and Chlum to Königgrätz and interned there. *En route* the escort that had been detached from IR 62 to guard the prisoners came under Prussian fire, which claimed five Prussian victims.

The attack of IR 6 on the woods and the village cost it 16 officers and nearly 400 soldiers. Among the dead were Captains Horváth and Voitel, *Oberlieutenants* Wachsmann and Schäfer, Lieutenants Klaudinger, *Baron* Codelli and Arseni, and 87 men.

In the [Austrian Staff work] *Österreichs Kämpfe in Jahre 1866*, the 2nd Battalion IR 6 is described as the battalion that delivered the attack on the Swiepwald. Also, on the map of the battlefield of Königgrätz [in the same work], '*Situation zu Mittag*' [Situation at Noon], the battalion indicated at the Máslowed–Cistoves sunken road is given the number 2/6 whereas on the map 'Situation vor der Einnahme des Ortes Chlum und Rozberic durch die preuß. 1. Garde – Division' [Situation before the Capture of Chlum and Rozberic by the Prussian 1st Guards Division] this battalion is given the number 1/6.

The first wave of Brigade Fleischhacker [together with the 1st Battalion and two divisions from IR 62 now occupied Cistoves]. The 1st Battalion IR 62 and the 6th division IR II/62 to the southwest, the 2nd Battalion IR 6, which had linked up with the 1st Battalion IR 6, and the 5th division IR II/62 to the north. The 3rd Battalion IR 6 established itself in the western part of the village and in the low ground to the west. All these units (which had become unavoidably intermingled) maintained intense fire against the 1st Battalion Pr. 27 and the 9th Company Pr. F/27 (which held their original position on the hillock directly northwest of Cistoves) as well as against the companies of the 2nd Battalion Pr. 27, which as mentioned above (according to Prussian sources) did not reach the southern margin of the woods until after the attack of the 1st Battalion IR 6 had been repelled.

At about this time, the attack of the Austrian 1st Feldjäger Battalion must also have taken place. This battalion (Brigade Benedek, 3rd Corps) was in the little wood between Chlum and Lípa when at about 10:00 a.m. its commanding officer (Major Kleinberg) was prompted by the General Staff Officer of Brigade Appiano (Captain Hegedüs) to advance with his battalion east of Cistoves and attack the Swiepwald. The attack was a complete failure however, and the battalion fell back and [rallied] next to Brigade Fleischhacker where it remained. The 1st division of the battalion later took part in the defence of the northern boundary of the woods and the 2nd division in the defence of the western side of Cistoves, while the 3rd division formed the reserve (but soon had to be brought up to reinforce the two other divisions). During the fighting in Cistoves, Lieutenant Polák was killed. Major Kleinberg, Captain Sedelmayer, Oberlieutenant Adj. Trevani, Oberlieutenant Pávek and Lieutenants Breitert and Fischer were all wounded.

In the meantime, the Prussian 1st Battalion Pr. 27 attacked Brigade Fleischhacker's left wing from the southern border of the Swiepwald. The battalion (which had become somewhat disorganised) was re-grouping at the southern border of the woods when Captain Schramm (who was now in command) looked [south] to see what lay beyond. In front of him he saw a low ridge and rising above it (to the west of Cistoves), the roofs of two farmsteads that belonged to the village. The ridge was held by an Austrian skirmish line, and farther to the rear there appeared to be units that were in close order. Nevertheless, Captain Schramm resolved to attack. The 1st and 4th Companies charged, and with significant losses reached the high ground from which the Austrian skirmish line had withdrawn. Now however, the Austrian batteries south of Máslowed took a hand in the matter and a hail of shells rained down (the Austrian infantry also opened fire). The two Prussian companies on the ridge suffered heavy losses and had to be pulled back into the woods, but the situation there was even worse. The shells continued to fall with unerring accuracy, not only from the left, but also from Chlum Hill to their front. It was impossible to remain there any longer so the 1st and 4th Companies advanced to the high ground (which in the meantime had been re-occupied by the Austrians) and captured it for the second time, while the two other companies of the 1st Battalion (the 2nd and 3rd) followed on. Once again, the battalion provided a superb target for infantry and artillery, resulting in frightful casualties.

At this critical juncture, the commander of the Prussian 14th Infantry Brigade, General von Gordon, appeared at the southwest corner of the Swiepwald. With him was Colonel von Bothmer, regimental commander of Pr. 67 (who had hurried from his 2nd Battalion) and the Adjutant of Pr. 27. The Adjutant was briefing the General on the situation when they suddenly came under fire from Austrian *Jägers*. Surprised by the fact that even though the whole of the 7th Division was already engaged, it was still possible for Austrian units to infiltrate as far as the western border, General von Gordon sent *his* Adjutant to Lieutenant General von Horn (commander of the Prussian 8th Division in the Skalka woods) with a request to support the 7th Division, whose forces he deemed insufficient to hold the entire Swiepwald.

General von Gordon then rode to the 1st Battalion Pr. 27 (which was still on the high ground) and had the 2nd and 3rd Companies (which were in close order and exposed to heavy Austrian fire) fall back to the edge of the woods. However, as had been the case with the 1st and 4th Companies, the hail of fire drove them back into the open [where they sought cover in a shallow hollow]. The battalion's situation grew increasingly critical, losses mounted, and it became obvious that it was absolutely impossible to remain there. Therefore, Captain Schramm decided to have the battalion attack the two farmsteads west of Cistoves [that he had spotted earlier from the edge of the woods]. That took place at 10:45 a.m.

Let us now return to Brigade Fleischhacker. While the first wave was hotly engaged with the 1st Battalion Pr. 27 west of Cistoves, the second wave conducted an extremely bloody attack against the southern border of the woods, unfortunately without the desired result.

Right after the capture of Cistoves by the first wave, the second wave (IR 61) formed in *Divisionsmassenlinie* with front facing the woods [north], 1st Battalion on the right, 3rd Battalion in the centre, and 2nd Battalion on the left. Even during its deployment the regiment suffered substantial losses. Then, preceded by a thin skirmish line and to the strains of the 'Radetzky March', the 1st and 3rd Battalions, echeloned from the left, began to advance (meantime, the brigade battery, from its position beside Cistoves, fired cannister at the edge of the woods). As soon as the signal for the assault sounded, the entire line charged.

According to the history of the Austrian 61st IR, the assault made it to the margin of the woods, however there is no mention of this in the Austrian or Prussian General Staff works, or in any of the various Prussian histories. According to statements in the regimental history of IR 61 (cited above), the course of the attack was as follows:

The 1st Battalion, under Major Villa, entered the woods with its first charge and drove the Prussian units positioned there back into the interior where they established themselves anew on a hill. The battalion then organised itself for defence in the sector that it had captured and held it in the murderous firefight that then developed.

The 3rd Battalion, under Lieutenant Colonel Gyurich, was initially exposed to heavy crossfire and had to fall back. The battalion commander, drilled through by two bullets, found a heroic death there, as did Captain Russ, commander of the 7th division. The battalion repeated its attack. Only on the third assault, delivered with great courage and bravery, was it able to force the Prussians back from the edge of the woods into the interior. In the course of this action *Oberlieutenant* Eichler and Captain Petrovi were wounded, the latter twice, one of which was serious.

The 2nd Battalion, commanded by Major Larisch, did not take part in the assault on the Swiepwald, but advanced against Cistoves, where it established itself in the northern sector.

The village of Cistoves in the middle ground. The southern border of the Swiepwald and the two knolls K and L are on the skyline Taken from the Cistoves – Koniggratz crossroads, at the monument to IR 49

Sadowa seen from the south west looking north east. The Swiepwald just visible on the right of the skyline

The regimental history goes on to say that while the fighting in the woods flowed indecisively back and forth, two battalions of Pr. 67 appeared by surprise and poured *schnellfeuer* into the right flank of that part of IR 61 that was in the woods. In order to avoid complete destruction, both battalions of IR 61 had to fall back behind Cistoves, where they were rallied by the regimental commanding officer, Colonel Bordolo.

The assertion that two battalions of Pr. 67 attacked the right flank of Brigade Fleischhacker's second wave cannot be reconciled with the facts. Each of the three battalions [of Pr. 67] were fighting in other parts of the woods. The Fusilier Battalion was in the north of the central sector B, the 1st Battalion on the ridge near the projection toward Másloved M, and the 2nd Battalion only emerged from the woods after the attack of Brigade Fleischhacker had already been repelled. Consequently, this must have been the place where (opposite the memorial to the Austrian 8th *Feldjäger* Battalion) a passing Prussian battalion could only have attacked the left, and not the right, flank. In any case, the Prussian companies fighting on the southern edge of the woods did receive timely help but not from the 67th, but rather from the 26th, whose 1st Battalion (as we already know) was in action at about 10:00 a.m. on Hill K. This was subsequently brought forward by Major Paucke (with three companies deployed to the southern boundary) where it plugged the gap between the 6th and 7th Companies Pr. II/27 at the very moment when the second wave of Brigade Fleischhacker launched its attack on the woods. Therefore, it must have been decisive in repelling that battalion's attack.

It seems quite remarkable that the platoon of *Premier Lieutenant* Haack (Pr. 27) was able to maintain its position (in the sunken road from Cistoves) even though the Austrian assault column passed near it but was repelled by *schnellfeuer*. In the regimental history of the Prussian 27th Infantry Regiment, the conduct of Brigade Fleischhacker's battery (Captain Kolárik, *Oberleutenant* Volkmer[2]) during the attack of the second wave of Brigade Fleischhacker is praised as follows: 'With admirable courage ['*defiance of death*' sic], the battery drove up to within a few hundred metres of the woods and poured shells and cannister into it.'

At about 11:00 a.m. the two battalions (2nd and 3rd) of IR 6 left Cistoves and joined the second wave, which then consisted of four battalions (1st and 3rd IR 61, and the 2nd and 3rd IR 6) positioned in the hollow east of Cistoves. The 1st Battalion IR 6 (less the 3rd division, which remained in the village) was still in the sunken road east of Cistoves facing the Swiepwald. The brigade battery went into position south of the hollow to the left of the second wave (the 7th Hussars *Prinz von Preussen*, had also taken position there) since it had suffered heavily from enemy artillery fire in its former position south of Másloved.

The village of Cistoves was held by the 2nd Battalion IR 61, the 1st Battalion IR 62, the 3rd division of IR 6 and the 1st *Feldjäger* Battalion. The 4th Company of the 13th *Feldjäger* Battalion, which fell back from the southeastern part of the Swiepwald toward Cistoves, and to which stragglers from other companies of that battalion had rallied, made its way to the right wing of Brigade Fleischhacker.

---

2   Captain Kolárik was awarded the *Orden der Eisernen Krone 3. Kl.* [Order of the Iron Crown, 3rd Class] and *Oberleutenant* Volkmer the *Militär-Verdienst-Kreuze (K.D.)* [Military Service Cross (K.D.)] by His Majesty. The latter officer later received repeated decorations for his outstanding conduct both in military and civil service. He attained the rank of a colonel in the reserves and was finally director of the *k.k. Staatsdruckerei* [Imperial Royal State Press] in Vienna. He died in 1901.

After the failure of the attack of IR 61, a period of relative calm settled over that part of the battlefield, but only briefly. Soon the fighting flared up again, this time with renewed intensity.

When it became impossible to remain on the ridge northwest of Cistoves any longer (due to heavy Austrian artillery and rifle fire), the Prussian 1st Battalion Pr. 27 launched the assault on the two isolated farmsteads southwest of Cistoves that had earlier been resolved upon by the battalion commander. This took place immediately before the attack of the first wave of Brigade Poeckh on the southeastern [Heidrich erroneously says the southwestern] border of the woods. The battalion was organised as follows: the 1st Company on the right, the 4th Company on the left, and the 2nd and 3rd Companies between and somewhat to their rear and formed as a half battalion. During the attack, the 1st Company took the western (right-hand) farmstead, while the 4th Company and the half battalion following it took the eastern (left-hand) farmstead as their objectives.

The 1st Company reached the western farmstead first without serious losses (it had been evacuated by the small Austrian garrison shortly before the attack and was further away from the flanking fire coming from Cistoves). The 4th Company on the other hand, suffered serious losses from heavy flanking fire from Cistoves as well as from frontal fire coming from the farmstead it was assaulting. The company (which had already been shaken by previous losses) faltered, but its commander, Lieutenant von Witzleben II, cheered his men on, whereupon they resumed the attack. As he neared the objective, however, Lieutenant von Witzleben was hit by three rifle bullets and knocked to the ground by a shell. Deprived of its leader for the second time, the company stopped short and wavered. This time Lieutenant von Lessel[3] sprang to the front and inspired the men so that they renewed their advance, and with a final charge reached the farmstead (which was surrounded by a garden). Since it was only defended by a few (mostly wounded) Austrian soldiers, the Prussians took it easily. Soon thereafter, the 2nd and 3rd Companies arrived having suffered less during their approach, even though they too had to advance without cover and under crossfire (Lieutenant von Ramdohr was seriously wounded in the right thigh by a shell fragment). The capture of these two farmsteads provided the Prussians with a base that would shortly become a rallying point for yet more of the 27th. It was 11:00 a.m.

Even though the Prussian 7th Division had been able to repel all the Austrian attacks on the woods so far, it was nevertheless in an extremely serious situation. The attack that Brigade Poeckh now delivered rendered that situation even worse.

Brigade Poeckh (which had deployed into battle formation southwest of Másloved) now received orders from Lieutenant Field Marshal Mollinary to attack the enemy occupying the woods opposite. Neither [Brigadier Poeckh nor his subordinate commanders] were given the necessary time to familiarise themselves with the terrain, [an elementary precaution] made all the more necessary due to the complete lack of good maps. The verbal order to launch an immediate assault was repeated and it had to be carried out. So it was that under the personal leadership of the Brigadier the first wave advanced without any preparatory fire (the deployment of skirmishers was dismissed as unnecessary so not a shot was fired) in total ignorance of [the enemy's strength or situation] or what would ensue from either the success or failure of the attack. The reply of Brigadier Poeckh to a question from the commanding officer of IR 51

---

3   The then Lieutenant von Lessel later attained the rank of Lieutenant General, and in 1900–1901 was the commander of the German infantry Division in East Asia.

Archduke Carl Ferdinand regarding the deployment of skirmishers is revealing. Upon hearing the question, Colonel Poeckh rode to within earshot of the regiment and cried out 'There are the woods, within it earn your Order of Theresa!'[4] Moreover, IR 37 (which formed the second wave) received no orders from the Brigadier concerning the timing or the direction of any possible support that it might be required to give. Yet the situation was by no means one in which it could be left without definite instructions, for as soon as the first wave entered the woods, it would be impossible for the second wave to follow the course of the action.

With great bravery, the four battalions of the first wave [three battalions of IR 51 on the right, the 8th *Feldjäger* Battalion on the left] launched their assault against the southeastern corner of the woods. However, as the advance proceeded it drifted to the right such that the right wing attacked the southeastern side of the woods without coming up against the 5th Company Pr. II/26 that was posted at the jutting angle of the eastern border T (where the memorial to the Austrian 13th *Feldjäger* Battalion now stands). The left wing, on the other hand, advanced directly northwards against the southern edge of the woods. The four battalions referred to above were followed by the 2nd Battalion IR 21 and the 1st Battalion IR 32nd [both left behind when 8th Corps moved south]. Despite the devastating enemy fire (both frontal and flanking) that tore serious gaps in their ranks, and despite the substantial problems caused by the broken terrain (they had to advance across two sunken roads and some very rough ground), the assault columns successfully reached the edge of the woods. The Prussian companies posted at the southern boundary of the woods fell back in every direction, all the while firing continuously and making good use of any available cover. Those of the 27th fell back primarily to the west, and some joined with the 1st Battalion Pr. 26 and retreated over the gently rising hill into the thicker woods behind.

The left wing of Brigade Poeckh thus achieved a degree of success, but not the right. As a result of the terrain difficulties described earlier, it reached the edge of the woods without significant losses but in a state of complete exhaustion. Fortunately for them the enemy was engaged with the 13th *Feldjäger* Battalion, while the 5th Company Pr. II/26 that was supposed to be defending that stretch of the woods, according to its own report, took no part in the fighting because it was totally unaware that it was taking place. Incredibly (as mentioned above) the Austrian 13th *Feldjäger* Battalion was still fighting on the slope T, while on the right flank, Captain Reichenbach (with 1½ companies) stood fast against Prussian attempts to envelop him (but at the cost of a shattered knee). It is truly amazing that this battalion stuck it out for so long, especially since the southern edge of the woods was already held by three Prussian companies (the 11th, 7th and 6th Companies Pr. 27), while to its rear, the Prussian 5th Company Pr. II/26 had gained a firm foothold. As can be seen, the situation of the [*Feldjägers*] should have been untenable, however the chaos that reigned everywhere, [the sound distortion], the thick mist and still thicker powder smoke often prevented either side from spotting the other until it was too late (if at all), and then of being able to respond appropriately. Many of the *impossible* things that happened in the Swiepwald can be explained by the *impossible* conditions.

In the interior of the woods, the totally exhausted Austrians [of Brigade Poeckh] made their arduous way along the slope T through thick young growth past the 13th *Feldjägers* (some of

---

4   Tr. Note – The Military Order of Maria Theresa was created by the Empress Maria in 1757 after the Battle of Kolin to reward commissioned officers for acts of exceptional courage, which *'might have been omitted by an honourable officer without reproach'.*

Cistoves (on fire)

Spire of Chlum Church

Prussian Infantry Regiment Nr. 26 Magdeburg standing on the track F - F facing south and firing into the flank of Brigade Poeckh which is attacking east to west across the cleared ares N The spire of Chlum church can he seen in the distance, Cistoves is on fire. From a painting by Ernst Zimmer. Print reproduced by kind permission of the Anne S.K. Brown Military Collection, Brown University Library.

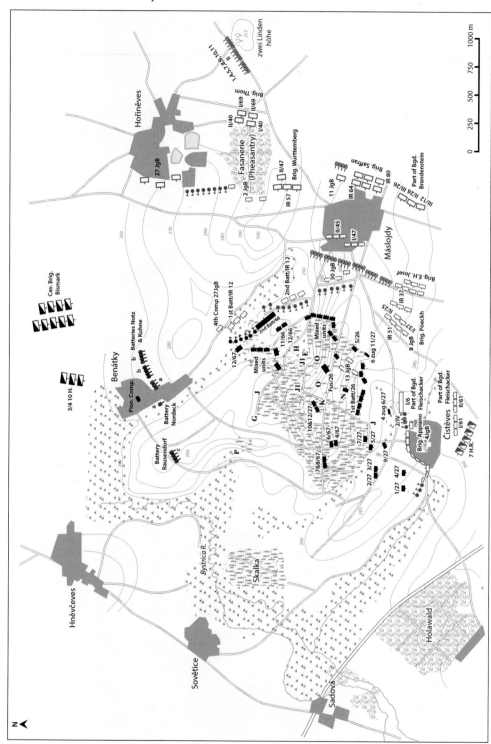

Map 2 The situation immediately before the attack of Brigade Poeckh 10:15 a.m.

whom joined them) to the low ground that stretched toward Cistoves. There the right wing came up against the 2nd Company Pr. I/67 as well as the Fusilier Battalion Pr. 26, the 9th Company Pr. F/66[5] and elements of the 1st Battalion Pr. 66 that were holding the steep slope. These Prussian forces, in conjunction with the 1st Battalion Pr. 26 which was falling back toward Hill K, received the attackers with fearsome crossfire.

This surprising turn of events, so favourable to the Prussians but so disadvantageous to the Austrians, had the following explanation. When the first wave of Brigade Poeckh captured the edge of the woods, skirmishers were sent forward who followed the retreating Prussians to the western border of the woods. Unfortunately however, this drew the attention of the attackers to the west and northwest. The ridge to their right, as well as the projection of the woods toward Másloved (both of which were held by the enemy), received less attention and it was from there that the disaster described originated. Contributing largely to this situation was the fact that before the columns had gone more than a few hundred paces into the woods, any overall command ceased. In the constant climbing and descending of slopes, in the immense drive to push forward through the thick brush, the assaulting troops were soon exhausted and their formations broken up. When they reached the bottom of the slope, the entire movement came to a halt. At this point Brigadier Poeckh decided to reorganise his forces, but suddenly and quite unexpectedly, enemy troops emerged to his right and rear, opening a murderous *schnellfeuer* on the massed Austrians and exacting enormous casualties. Fearful confusion developed, the tenuous contact between formations was totally lost, tactical cohesion dissolved and the issuance of orders ceased since nearly all the staff officers and senior captains as well as large numbers of the other officers, were killed or wounded. Brigadier Colonel Poeckh was severely wounded (he was later found by a patrol of the Prussian 67th and brought to a dressing station where he subsequently died).

Despite everything, the battalions continually pressed forward. The Prussians, who could not withstand the weight of the attack, abandoned the ridge crest and the knoll, and were for the most part forced down off the slope. They soon rallied however, and reinforced by the many

---

5   Tr. Note – The author (possibly the typesetter) has erroneously written 'the 9th Company 63rd Infantry Regiment'; however, the Prussian 63rd IR was not involved in the Battle of Königgrätz. According to the Order of Battle of the Prussian 2nd Army given by von Moltke, the 4. *Oberschlesische Infanterie* Regt. Nr. 63, which had originally been assigned to the garrison of Neisse, later joined the Detachment of *Generalmajor* von Knobelsdorff in its defence of the eastern Silesian border region. (Helmuth von Moltke, *Moltkes Militärische Werke II, Die Thätigkeit als Chef des Generalstabes der Armee im Frieden, Moltkes Taktisch-Strategisch Aufsätze aus den Jahren 1857 bis 1871: Memoire an Seine Majestät den König vom 25 Juli 1868 über die bei der Bearbeitung des Feldzuges 1866 hervorgetretenen Erfahrungen*, and *Betrachtunge vom Frühjahre 1867 über Konzentrationen im Kriege von 1866* (Berlin: Ernst Siegfried Mittler und Sohn, 1900)). Examination of Heidrich's second map, *Plan des Svib-Waldes vom Jahre 1866, Situation umnmittelabar vor dem Angriffe der Brigade Poeckh um 10:15 vorm.* shows the 9th Company of the 66th in a position where it would have become involved with the advance of the first wave of Brigade Poeckh. Gaertner, in his *Die ersten 15 Jahre des 3. Magdeburgischen Infanterieregiments Nr. 66*, describes how, at *Oberstlieutenant* von Hochstetter's request, *Premier Lieutenant* von Gneist, who wished to join with Hochstetter's three companies in attacking the advancing Brigade Poeckh, instead held his 9th Company back while Hochstetter attacked with his three companies of the 67th so as to permit them a passage through the lines of the 9th Company in the event their attack was repelled. (Richard Gaertner, *Die ersten 15 Jahre des 3. Magdeburgischen Infanterie-regiments Nr. 66* (London: Wentworth Press, 2019), p.87).

units that hurried there from other parts of the woods, fell on the Austrian flanks and rear, all the while making good use of their [quick firing] rifle. So, it came about, that the initially victorious Brigade Poeckh ended up in such difficulties. Its general staff officer, Captain Klobus, attempted to reach IR 37 with the order to advance, but he could no longer get through because in the meantime the enemy had infiltrated between the two waves, thereby severing communications. Under attack from all sides, cut down in droves by the devastating effect of the enemy's fire, disorientated and cut off from its reserves, the isolated Austrians fought on in the woods for a full two hours in the hope of finding a way out. Only a few managed to escape however, since most of those that reached the western and northwestern borders of the woods fell into the hands of the two freshly arrived battalions of the enemy's 8th Division. Some of the individual actions of Brigade Poeckh are described below.

The divisions of the 8th *Feldjäger* Battalion that were advancing on the left wing and the 1st Battalion IR 32, changed front after entering the southern edge of the woods and advanced towards the west, as did the 2nd Battalion IR 21. The divisions of IR 51 on the other hand, advanced partly in that direction and partly towards the north and northwest. The 1st division that formed the extreme right flank of IR 51 had already gone 500 paces into the woods when the previously mentioned Prussian ambush took place. The division marched to the right and opened up brisk fire against the enemy, maintaining its position for nearly two hours despite the fact that the 1st Company alone lost two officers and 61 men. Only when the division was fired on from the rear (it was now surrounded on three sides) did it abandon its former position in order to escape capture. The 1st Company then fell back to the south of the woods, stormed a section of the perimeter (that had in the meantime been occupied by the enemy) and held it open until the rest of the regiment under Major Bartha had passed through.

The 2nd, 3rd, and 4th divisions of IR 51 advanced toward the knoll K in the middle of the woods where they came up against elements of the 1st Battalion Pr. 26, as well as the 10th and 12th Fusilier Companies Pr. 27, which they drove off. Later however (as a result of the density of the woods and enemy action), these divisions became separated and fought on in isolation.

The 2nd division (which included the Colours of the 1st Battalion) was gradually smashed to the point where only the colour bearer, *Fahnenführer* Nagy,[6] and the colour officer, *Fahnen Officier Oberleutnant* Kovacic, remained. After much stumbling around in the woods, and surviving many trials and tribulations, often under heavy enemy fire, these two finally found their way out and reached the regiment's rallying point.

The 5th and 6th divisions, like the 7th, 8th, and 9th, advanced toward the west. The first two made it to the western edge of the woods, where only a few men escaped. The 7th, 8th and 9th divisions initially advanced in good order but were later thrown into disarray, partly by friendly troops retreating through their ranks and partly by surprise enemy flank attacks. Isolated groups made it to the western edge of the woods where they were either killed or captured by the enemy. When Major Bartha realised he was the [senior] surviving officer of IR 51, he made renewed efforts to rally his terribly disorganised men. After lengthy searching, he found a gully about 300 paces long that was surrounded by tall trees. Here he had the 'Halt'

---

6   *Fahnenführer* Nagy was still active in the regiment at the time this book was written. He was present as a member of the regimental deputation that attended the ceremony of consecration of the monument in honour of the regiment's fallen, that was erected by the officer's corps in September 1902.

and the 'Cease Fire' blown, thereby drawing to himself all the members of IR 51 who were in the vicinity. A quick reconnaissance revealed an adjoining area of young growth that was only weakly held by the enemy. Major Bartha realised that if there was to be any chance of escape, it would have to be there, and he hurried back to the rallying point where in the meantime (under the protection of a flank detachment) more men had assembled. Major Bartha then began the retreat [towards the weakly held area], however the situation was complicated by a broad, rocky ditch that divided the gully in which they were sheltering. Suddenly firing broke out to the rear, and the troops on the right of the ditch followed Major Bartha while those on the far side were driven toward the enemy and were scattered or taken prisoner, of which more will be said later.

Major Bartha broke through the enemy lines with what remained of the regiment (20 officers and about 900 men), supported by the survivors of the 1st Company (that was retreating towards the southeast). He rallied them near the second wave (that had remained outside the woods) where they were joined by the remnants of the other three battalions of the first wave. It is likely that many of the 51st that had advanced to the north or west of the woods and become separated heard Major Bartha's signal, but their efforts to rejoin the regiment were mostly in vain. Driven back and forth by the enemy and generally worn down, they were reduced to small groups and were for the most part captured.

During the fighting described above, the Colours of the 2nd and 3rd Battalions of IR 51 fell into enemy hands. After the colour officers had fallen, the colour bearers of these battalions wandered around in the woods, initially alone but later joined by other small groups. One platoon of the enemy's Pr. 72 came upon such a wandering group that included the colours of the 2nd Battalion IR 51. During the fierce fighting that ensued, the colour bearer, *Fahnenführer* Szilágyi, was shot and a Prussian Musketeer leaped forward and tore the colours from the hands of the dying man. The other Austrians could not come to his assistance since they were either felled or captured.

Fahnenführer Hederich, with the colours of the 3rd Battalion IR 51, joined up with another group, but unable to go any further due to exhaustion he collapsed. Colour bearer Götzmann of the 16th Company then took the colours and joined some of the regiment led by Lieutenant Pilarský, but at the very moment the Lieutenant took the colours from him a [shell] shattered Götzmann's shoulder and soon thereafter the officer was wounded as well. The little group of the 51st (which had rallied around their colours) was finally reduced to one officer and 25 men. Gradually, bit by bit, stragglers from other Austrian units joined them and increased their number to 150. Exhausted and nearly incapable of fighting, they proceeded in a direction diametrically opposite to the line of retreat [and emerged from the northern edge of the wood where they encountered a squadron of the Prussian 10th Hussars]. Worn out and entirely without ammunition, they were left with no alternative but to surrender. It is interesting to note that the little group in question brought a small number of Prussian soldiers along with them as prisoners, including two non-commissioned officers of the 2nd Company Pr. I/72. As soon as one of these caught sight of the Prussian Hussars (before the latter could even attack), he threw himself on the Austrian Colour bearer and tore the Colours from his grasp. In the meantime, the Hussars charged into the midst of the developing struggle, grabbed the Colours for themselves and galloped off. The Prussian account, whereby an entire battalion of the Austrian 51st with Colours present and weapons extended [surrendered to] the Prussian 10th Hussars bears little resemblance to the facts and is based on a lie.

The history of the Austrian IR 21 [Brigade Wöber, 8th Corps, left behind when 8th Corps re-deployed to the south] states that during the assault on the Swiepwald its 2nd Battalion followed directly behind the right wing of IR 51 [however, the author states earlier, 'The 2nd Battalion IR 21and the 1st Battalion IR 32 closed up behind the left wing of the first wave']. After capturing the edge of the woods, the first wave resumed its assault on the dense, strongly held interior, but suffered substantial losses from heavy rifle fire (from its left flank and rear) and began to waver and retire (this may have been the 'moment' referred to in *Österreichs Kämpfe im Jahre 1866* when the advance came to a halt). Major von Fischer (commanding officer, 2nd Battalion IR 21) noticed the first wave's hesitancy and had the 'Assault' sounded to hasten the advance of his own men. As the wavering elements [of the 51st] became aware of the advance of the 21st, they took heart and renewed their attack with fresh courage, finally succeeding in taking the woods.

Because the first wave initially bore off to the right, contact with the left was broken, from which direction the Prussians still maintained a brisk flanking fire. To curtail it, the 7th Company was deployed into a firing line, while Major von Fischer and his battalion (which had already been seriously depleted by the heavy losses sustained at Skalitz) overwhelmed the enemy in front and forced them to retreat. This advance brought the battalion into the first line with the 51st on its right and the 1st Battalion IR 32 on its left. The Prussians did not hold their ground and retreated. However, when the Austrian assault column reached the swampy low ground that led to Cistoves, it was forced back by a sudden storm of rifle fire delivered at close range from the steep slope diagonally opposite its right flank. In the resulting confusion, some of the 51st that were retreating forced their way through the weaker 21st, splitting it into two parts. The enemy drove one part before it to the west, and the other retired to the northwest.

In the enfilade described above, both the Battalion Commander (Major von Fischer) and his Adjutant had their horses shot from beneath them. When the Major (still dazed from his fall) raised himself from the ground, he found only his Adjutant, the colour bearer and about ten men at his side, while (as a result of the temporary loss of command) the remainder of the battalion had stormed forward. Some of the battalion (fighting constantly) successfully made it to the western edge of the woods, but their retreat was then barred by the Prussians who closed in behind them.

A large part of the left wing was either killed or captured, while a part of the right wing (led by *Oberlieutenant* Lesonitzky), together with some stragglers from the first wave, desperately tried to fight their way out. Battling tirelessly, this group made its way from the northwest corner of the woods to the sector marked M that bulged towards Másloved. There, on the third attempt, they finally broke through and into the open, however to reach the Másloved–Nedelišt road required more effort and more losses. From there *Oberlieutenant* Lesonitzký led the remnants of the battalion (four officers and 42 men) to Nedelišt, and then to Charbusic, where at about 4:00 p.m. they were reunited with the rest of the regiment.

Major von Fischer and his faithful men also tried to escape from the woods but they were not so lucky. Closely encircled by some of the Prussian 72nd and without hope of escape, he and his Adjutant disappeared into the thick undergrowth with the colour bearer where they broke the flagstaff into pieces and concealed the colours beneath his [Major von Fischer's] clothing.[7] A few moments later they were taken prisoner.

---

7   On the occasion of the march of the prisoner transport through Jicin. Major von Fischer, since he felt very weak and feared that he would be turned over to an enemy hospital, entrusted the colours to a former member of the regiment who lived there, Sergeant Anton Cech. On his return from captivity

The regimental history of IR 32 gives more details of the 1st Battalion's battle:

Along with the 2nd Battalion IR 21, the battalion formed the second wave behind the 51st. When after a brief firefight the edge of the woods was taken by assault, the advance to the large clearing [that is, the southern cleared area N] began. Since the Prussians had taken position on the far side of the clearing, the battalion was brought up from the second to the first line and after short period of preparatory rifle fire, the attack was made, the enemy forced back, and many prisoners taken. The commander of the battalion, Major von Kronenfels, was seriously wounded in the attack.

During the further advance of the brigade, the 51st came under volley fire at extremely short range which forced part of it to retire. As they retreated they ran into the 1st Battalion IR 32 and disrupted it. From that point on, all organised fighting ceased. The main body of the battalion soon re-assembled, but on account of the many obstacles to movement, individual groups were again separated or became mixed up with other Austrian formations. Completely disorientated, not knowing which way to turn, here the Austrians captured a body of Prussians, there the Prussians captured a body of Austrians, until finally, reinforced by fresh battalions, the Prussians gained the upper hand. Fired on from all sides in this *melée*, the battalion lost most of its effectives. A small, tight-knit remnant of 39 men, led by *Oberlieutenants* Andreanezký and Magistris, more dead than alive and unable to use their rifles because they had become wet, emerged from the edge of the woods and surrendered to a squadron of Prussian Hussars that had encircled them. The capture of this little group must have taken place at the same time as those from the 51st, which was under Lieutenant Pilarský's command. Captain Hussa was the only officer who, by a miracle, escaped the disaster. A very few of the men were fortunate in saving themselves. The colours of the battalion were lost in the confusion. Where and how is unknown.'

The actions of the 8th *Feldjäger* Battalion cannot be described in detail because the history of this battalion contains nothing significant in this respect. Prussian reports describe the effect that the first wave of Brigade Poeckh's attack had on them. It was said that the assault by Brigade Poeckh initially hit the 6th Platoon of the 11th Company Pr. F/27 (positioned at the southeastern corner of the woods), which in the hand-to-hand fighting that ensued was thrown back and scattered. As the attack continued, the weight of the assault fell on the 11th Company's flank, which despite firing desperately was also scattered, some being forced further into the woods where they were tossed back and forth by the growing swell of the battle. A few Fusiliers were driven all the way back to the opposite side of the woods, where on the track by Cistoves (behind which the assault passed without hitting them) they came to a halt and found fresh courage with *Premier Lieutenant* Haack's steadfast platoon. The battalion's colours were saved with extreme difficulty.

Poeckh's overwhelmingly superior force then rolled onwards towards the 6th and 7th Companies Pr. II/27 where again it hit them in the flank. The skirmishers that were at the edge of the woods were driven off after only weak resistance. Those that had established themselves

to Vienna in September 1866, he presented the colours that had thus been saved to Archduke Albrecht.

farther forward met the same fate and barely escaped capture in the bitter hand-to-hand fighting that followed. The four platoons of these two companies that had been positioned in the woods as supports were simply tossed aside (to the west) by the powerful shock. Many Musketeers were reduced to wandering around aimlessly, and some were temporarily captured while others linked up with larger groups from the adjoining battalion.

After the three companies of the Prussian 27th were defeated, the assault struck the 1st Battalion of the 26th which did no better than the 27th. The Prussians were fortunate however, the 2nd Battalion Pr. 67 now arrived to oppose Brigade Poeckh, and before long they were joined by the 4th *Jäger* Battalion and the 1st Battalion Pr. 72.

It should probably be stated at this point that the description of the attack of Brigade Poeckh that appears in the regimental history of the Prussian 26th Infantry Regiment cannot be entirely reconciled with the facts. In the regimental history, the attack of the first wave is described at great length, followed by that of the second wave (supposedly IR 37). If we recall that the second wave did not in fact follow the first, and that the first took place more than two hours later [than the time stated in the regimental history] and under entirely different circumstances, we are forced to conclude that what the above history described as the first wave was actually the attack of the Austrian 1st *Feldjäger* Battalion [Brigade Benedek, 3rd Corps], which took place immediately *before* the attack of Brigade Poeckh. Since attacks were also conducted from Cistoves against the southern margin of the woods by isolated units of Brigade Fleischhacker (immediately after the major attack described above), it is presumed likely that these attacking units were also reported as belonging to Brigade Poeckh.

As already stated, the 1st Battalion Pr. 26 was driven from the edge of the woods by the first wave of Brigade Poeckh (as were the 11th, 6th, and 7th Companies Pr. 27) and fell back to the knoll K in the centre of the woods where it halted and took part in further fighting.

Again and again, the attackers directed their assault against the Prussians who were holding the southern margin of the woods. In the meantime, the main body of the 6th and 7th Companies Pr. II/27 were forced back behind the 5th and 8th Companies (of the same battalion) by the immense pressure of the Austrian columns that were close on their heels. The two former companies [the 6th and 7th] emerged from the woods into the open on the far side of the Benátek–Cistoves road, on which the vanguard of the 2nd Battalion Pr. 67 could be seen approaching. Major General Gordon who was nearby (he had just come from the attack of the 1st Battalion Pr. 27 on the farmsteads west of Cistoves) ordered them to follow that battalion.

When the above-mentioned [6th and 7th] companies (battered, bruised, and significantly reduced by losses and straggling) reached the hill west of Cistoves, they were deluged by a fearsome rain of shells from the Austrian batteries, heavy fire to their flank from Cistoves and to their rear from the Austrian 8th *Feldjägers* (who were lining the edge of the woods). The latter (who comprised the left wing of Brigade Poeckh) had already pressed forward far beyond the Benátek–Cistoves road. Beset from every direction, the two Prussian companies were forced to go the only way that permitted escape from their desperate situation, namely to the west. By this stage the advancing columns of the 8th Division were already visible, but as the shattered remnants headed towards them they came under fire from a Prussian battery that was positioned south of the Skalka woods and were forced back to the highway. Following that, they finally reached the Holáwald where they caught their breath and re-grouped. By now the two companies had lost more than half their complement.

The left wing of Brigade Poeckh advanced along the edge of the woods where it encountered the 8th Company Pr. II/27 (which at that moment had been joined by the Regimental Commander, Colonel von Zychlinski). Here the attack amounted to an envelopment and the 8th Company (who had been exposed to heavy Austrian shell and rifle fire) and adjoining 9th Company now came under serious fire from the rear. Losses were substantial. The 8th Company, which had already been badly mauled, received the full force of the 8th *Feldjäger*'s assault and was scattered, one part being driven into the woods and another towards the 9th Company of the same regiment, which was still holding firm.

The 5th Company Pr. II/27 (behind which this attack advanced) continued to hold its position at the southern margin of the woods, west of the Benátek–Cistoves road. Colonel Zychlinski (who was close by) immediately realised the seriousness of the situation and that retreat was all but impossible. He therefore ordered the company to break out towards the two farmsteads west of Cistoves and then hurried over to the 9th Company to give it the same instruction. At this moment the 9th Company came under heavy fire to its flank from Cistoves and to its rear from the woods. The company commander, Captain von Buddenbrock, was seriously wounded. About 40 Fusiliers rallied round him while the rest of the company (including Lieutenant Colonel von Zedwitz, Major von Busse and several other officers) under the personal leadership of Colonel von Zychlinski (who was shot through the thigh in the course of this action), hurried towards the farmstead that was farthest [to the west] from Cistoves (it had previously been taken by the 1st Company).

Soon General von Gordon also arrived there and a bit later Lieutenant von Carlowitz, the adjutant of the Fusilier Battalion, along with a group of stragglers he was leading. After the 8th Company had been scattered, the Adjutant gathered a number of Fusiliers from all four companies, which he then led against an Austrian battery that appeared nearby (probably that of Brigade Fleischhacker). He pushed forwards towards the road but extremely heavy, point-blank rifle fire limited his further advance. Turning now towards the farmstead mentioned above, he had to run a veritable gauntlet of fire between Cistoves on one side and the woods on the other. Making haste to the place where earlier the 8th Company Pr. II/27 had stood, he noticed that the 2nd Battalion Pr. 67 (which had just arrived) had forced its way into the midst of Brigade Poeckh and was advancing with a deployed skirmish line toward Cistoves. In the meantime the 5th Company Pr. II/27 also left the woods and headed for the same farmstead that the 2nd, 3rd, and 4th Companies already occupied. Rifles crackled on all sides, man after man sank to the ground, Musketeers staggered and fell, but persevering through the murderous fire, they too made it to the farm.

It was after 11:00 a.m. The commander of the Prussian 9th Company Pr. F/27, Captain von Buddenbrock (surrounded by a few of his Fusiliers), was lying wounded in a cornfield west of the hill that he had held for so long when he saw an Austrian *Feldjäger* battalion (the 8th) emerge from the woods and prepare to attack. Despite the Fusilier's rapid fire the *Feldjägers* charged, but unfortunately for them, shells from the Austrian batteries at Másloved (who had mistaken the *Feldjäger* for a Prussian column breaking out of the woods) smashed into their ranks. Captain von Buddenbrock described the fearsome effect of this fire: 'The battalion was nearly wiped out, reluctantly accepting the necessity of retreat it had to fall back, but still held its position at the edge of the woods.'

Captain von Buddenbrock had so far looked in vain for a friendly body of troops. His gaze now turned to the west where (at the same time the Austrian *Feldjäger* were retreating) he saw two

Prussian battalions moving eastwards. Soon the 1st Company Pr. I/72 [8th Division] arrived, thus relieving the little Fusilier detachment from its desperate predicament. The Prussian 10th and 12th Companies Pr. F/27 that were on the track north of Hill K were also impacted by the advance of Brigade Poeckh. The 10th Company was totally shattered, some fleeing south where they ran into the 8th Company at the very moment when it too had to fall back before the shock of the assault. A few people rallied around the Adjutant, Lieutenant von Carlowitz, who was at that moment attempting a breakthrough, while others joined up with the remnants of the 9th Company and thereby made it to the protection of the farmstead west of Cistoves. Still others however, caught up in the fearsome confusion of the forest, stumbled around for a lengthy time until, exhausted and broken, they made it to Benátek at about 12:00 p.m. Yet more wandered aimlessly through the woods, were captured, freed again, and hunted back and forth, barely surviving dangers only to suffer yet new misfortunes.

The mighty assault of Brigade Poeckh struck the 12th Company Pr. F/27 like a hurricane and smashed it to pieces, leaving the survivors to stagger out of the woods towards Benátek where they joined the men of the 9th and 11th Companies. The remnants of these four Fusilier companies were consolidated into a single detachment and employed to garrison the village. This happened at about 12:00 p.m. The attack of Brigade Poeckh had a similar effect on the other Prussian units that it struck. The tactical cohesion of the 1st Battalion Pr. 26 had already been loosened defending the edge of the woods and as the companies were forced back towards the interior, the ebb and flow of the fighting only increased their confusion.

Following the attack on the Prussian flank, the battalion commander, Major Paucke, received orders from Lieutenant General von Fransecky to fall back to Benátek with his battalion, of which only two platoons of the 3rd Company (which had seen relatively little of the fighting) were still in reasonably good order. To these were joined another two newly formed platoons, which had been hastily reconstituted from men of the other companies. At about 11:00 a.m. Major Paucke led his four platoons (which included the colours) towards Benátek (Lieutenant General Fransecky was seeking to avert the impending envelopment of his left wing by occupying the village). From those fragments of the battalions still capable of fighting, and by incorporating stragglers from other regiments of the Division, Captains Westerhagen I and Horn similarly reconstituted two new companies that went back into action somewhat later.

Let us now examine the actions of those Prussian formations that were positioned on the ridge, during and after the attack of Brigade Poeckh. It was the 1st Battalion Pr. 67, whose 2nd Company first saw the three battalions [the first wave] of Brigade Poeckh advancing across the slope towards their deployed platoon. Soon the platoon (completely enveloped and under fire from the rear) was left with no alternative but to fall back to the north as rapidly as possible. The other two platoons of the company withdrew farther to the right (westwards) to the spine road from Másloved [F–F], where on their left, groups of Pr. 26 were already engaged [well depicted in the print by Zimmer which appears at the beginning of the book]. When the Austrian attack columns [came into range], the two platoons rushed forward over the road and took up positions behind the piles of cordwood, from which they could cover the slope to their front N. From this position they maintained a heavy fire on the Austrian 13th *Feldjäger* that were facing them but it was impossible to advance further. Soon afterwards the company was attacked in front and flank by another Austrian column and pursued by heavy fire, was forced to retreat westwards. After much wandering it reached the northern boundary of the woods where the company commander, Captain Drigalski, gathered them together behind the Fusilier Battalion of its own regiment and prepared to renew the battle.

In the course of their advance, some of Brigade Poeckh (that were pursuing the 2nd Company Pr. I/67) got into the rear of the 3rd and 4th Companies that were at the [eastern] end of the northern slope and forced them to descend into the sunken meadow. However, finding themselves totally isolated there, they had to retreat further north until they made it to the central sector B, where they took up a position to the left of the Fusilier Battalion Pr. 67 and joined them in the fighting.

It was 11:00 a.m. The 9th and 10th Companies Pr. F/26 (which, as mentioned previously, had fallen back behind the 2nd Battalion of their own regiment after the failed attack on Másloved) fought the right wing of Brigade Poeckh from the ridge but were forced back to the northern margin of the woods and then pushed out, where they were ordered by Lieutenant General Fransecky to fall back on Benátek. The 11th and 12th Companies commanded by Captain Boltenstern (after their flank attack against Brigade Poeckh) reached the southern edge of the woods where they were soon involved in fresh fighting.

Only three units of the Prussian 66th opposed the advance of Brigade Poeckh. The first was the rifle platoon of the 11th Company (Lieutenant Platten), which was initially positioned west of Hill K and then fell back on the 2nd Battalion Pr. 67 at the southern margin of the woods. To its east, on the upper part of the southern cleared area N, was the 9th Company (minus its rifle platoon) under *Premier Lieutenant* Gneist, with front facing southeast. Close to that was the rifle platoon of the 12th Company under Lieutenant von Westernhagen. These latter two (the 9th and 12th companies) were thrown off the hill at the same time as the 9th and 10th Companies Pr. F/26 and driven into the pole woods, whereupon they left the woods at the northern boundary and later came into action on the meadow. There were also numerous small encounters between units of the Prussian 66th and 67th and stragglers from Brigade Poeckh.

It is now time to describe the fighting between isolated units of Brigade Poeckh and the 2nd Battalion Pr. 67 that was positioned near Cistoves. As noted previously, the 2nd Battalion Pr. 67 appeared opposite Cistoves at the same time as the companies of Pr. 27 (that were situated at the southern margin of the woods) were rolled up by the left wing of Brigade Poeckh. Immediately thereafter, parts of Brigade Fleischhacker attacked the southern margin of the woods from Cistoves, however they were driven off by the *schnellfeuer* of the 67th. (Captain Hirschfeld of the 1st Company fell in that action, and Captain Hergass of the 8th Company received two wounds, shot through the neck and shoulder.) The 67th then broke out from the edge of the woods on its own and advanced over the meadow as far as the orchard way. The 8th Company remained in the meadow as support, while the other three companies deployed and took cover behind a high bank (a field boundary), from where they opened a brisk fire on the village. After some time, Austrian troops were seen advancing against both flanks of the battalion. These troops must have been from Brigade Fleischhacker as well as from Brigade Poeckh (having lost their bearings in the woods), both had been involved in heavy fighting and were by no means the 'fresh battalions' referred to in the regimental history of the Prussian 67th Infantry Regiment.

In response to the impending attack, the battalion changed its formation. The rifle platoon of the 6th Company, with a half platoon of the 8th Company (which also included the colours), went back to the edge of the woods. The 7th Company (formerly under Captain Laue, now under Lieutenant Vorberg) remained with its front facing Cistoves. The rest of the 6th Company and the 1st Company had to cover the left flank of the battalion, while the 2½ platoons of the 8th

Schloss →

Maierhof →

The village of Horenoves seen from the south looking north.

Chlum church spire

The Pheasantry at Horenoves

View of the village of Máslowed and the pheasantry at Horenoves (from the north east).

Company covered the right flank. The 1st and 6th Companies (a total of four platoons) then attacked the advancing Austrians [whose organisation seems to have been somewhat disrupted as the author describes them as attacking in *bunches*] and forced them to retreat from the *schnell-feuer*. In this action, *Premier Lieutenant* and battalion Adjutant Kummer, Lieutenant von Jagove of the 1st Company and Lieutenant Leue of the 6th Company were killed. Captain Müller of the 1st Company received minor wounds.

According to the regimental history of Pr. 67, the colours of the 3rd Battalion IR 38 *Graf Haugwitz* were captured in this affair. If one considers that no part of IR 38 (let alone an entire battalion with its colours) was engaged on this part of the battlefield, and moreover that the regiment in question (as part of 1st Corps) went into position in its entirety at Rosnitz, and only in the afternoon after the capture of Chlum by the Prussian Guards Corps took part in the attack against the hill, then it is clearly out of the question that its 3rd Battalion could have lost its colours before noon, let alone at the southern border of the Swiepwald. Even though this is not the place to explain or correct such errors, it seems appropriate to at least make mention of it. The colours that were captured at the southern edge of the Swiepwald after 11:00 a.m. must in all likelihood have belonged to the 1st Battalion IR 32 *d'Este*, and to have fallen into Prussian hands in the same manner as did the two colours of IR 51. It seems worth noting that there is no mention of the capture of the colours of the 1st Battalion IR 32 in any Prussian account of the fighting in the Swiepwald. In the history of the Prussian 26th Infantry Regiment it says that the Prussian 7th Division captured two colours, which no doubt refers to those of IR 51.

In the meantime, the fighting along the southern border of the Swiepwald raged on.

[While the 1st and 6th companies Pr. 67 were attacking the Austrians on the left], the 8th Company Pr. II/67 also attacked the Austrians on the right, but it was pushed into the woods and scattered. A number of stragglers (under Lieutenant Kunze) joined up with a company of Pr. 72, while others (under Lieutenant *Graf* Westarp) found employment later as prisoner escorts. The Austrians established themselves firmly at the edge of the woods, however they would soon be engaged with the two battalions of the Prussian 8th Division that were hurrying to the support the 7th.

The rifle platoon of the 6th Company Pr. II/67 that was positioned on the southern border of the woods, together with a half platoon of the 8th Company (accompanied by Major von Zedwitz, the battalion commander), formed a defensive front against the enveloping Austrians, but becoming in danger of being flanked (on the right), fell back to the junction of the Másloved – Cistoves – Benátek roads [F–F W–W]. There it stopped (behind a small knoll that was not covered with trees) and opened up on the advancing Austrians to prevent them from debouching from the woods. Major Zedwitz succeeded in repelling the further attacks of IR 51 and the 8th *Feldjägers* on his left flank and to maintain his position until the fighting in the forest had ended. After the 8th Company and the rifle platoon of the 6th Company Pr. II/67 had been forced back [from their initial position, see above], only two platoons each of the 1st and 6th Companies, as well as the entire 7th Company Pr. 67 remained. The latter continued to hold the same position at the orchard way that it had held since the start of the fighting. In conjunction with the platoon of *Premier Lieutenant* Haack (Pr. 27) that was still on its left and which had been substantially reinforced with stragglers from other companies, as well as with a group on its right that had also been formed from stragglers (mostly from Pr. 27, about 150 men strong), it kept up heavy fire against the Cistoves garrison. These three Prussian units not only maintained their position for a long time, but even gained small temporary advantages, which will be described later.

As the above account indicates, the Prussians had been almost entirely driven out of the southern part of the woods by 11:00 a.m. Small groups of Prussians and Austrians continued to wander around in confusion, which resulted in numerous encounters. The Prussians still held the southern tip of the projection of the woods toward Másloved M, as well as the western sector C, the central sector B and the Havranec A. However, not only had the ranks of their battalions been seriously thinned, but their organisation was also badly affected.

Accordingly, at the same time the 1st Battalion Pr. 27 debouched from the southwestern margin of the woods (probably at about 10:15 a.m. as noted above) the commander of the Prussian 14th Infantry Brigade [General von Gordon] appealed to the commander of the Prussian 8th Division, Lieutenant General von Horn, for reinforcements, which were promised and immediately dispatched. If the 7th Division had not been reinforced at this extremely critical time, the fate of Brigade Poeckh (or what was left of it) would probably have been entirely different and the attack of Brigades Württemberg and Saffran, which took place shortly thereafter, would not have been so costly.

If, as we shall see later, the final success of the Austrian forces was modest, it could have been attained much earlier and significantly easier than it was. At the very moment General von Horn's divisional reserve was withdrawing to the Holáwald, the 1st Battalion Pr. 72 and the 4th *Jäger* Battalion were ordered to hurry to the aid of their hard-pressed sister Division in the Swiepwald. This took place shortly before 11:00 a.m.

The 1st Battalion Pr. 72 (initially positioned south of Sovetic) completed its deployment under cover of the Skalka woods and then set out for the westernmost tip of the Swiepwald that projects the farthest towards Sadová (where the road from Másloved joins the Benátek–Cistoves road that passes to the west of the woods). During its advance the battalion came under heavy fire from the Austrian batteries positioned at Lípa and suffered several casualties. (Lieutenant Kramer was killed and Captain Plötz was severely wounded.) The 1st Company on the right and the 4th Company on the left (preceded by skirmishers) formed the first wave, followed about 100 paces behind by the 2nd and 3rd Companies as a half battalion in close order. Received with weak volleys by the scattered relics of Brigade Poeckh that were lining the western edge of the woods, the two Prussian companies stormed forward and forced the Austrians back (the Austrians were exhausted and frequently fighting without officers). The rifle platoon of the 1st Company (Lieutenant Michler) pursued a group of the Austrian 8th *Feldjägers* towards the southern margin of the woods. It then took position west of the Benátek–Cistoves road and linked up there with about 100 stragglers from the 27th and 67th regiments (taking part in the fighting against the Austrians in and around Cistoves). It also attacked the battery of Brigade Fleischhacker, but in vain, later rejoining its own company which had in the meantime re-grouped not far from that location.

Captain Hanstein (the commander of the 1st Company) followed a different course with his other two platoons. He proceeded farther to the right (south) and as mentioned above, reached the southern margin of the woods at the Benátek–Cistoves road near the 9th Company Pr. F/27. There he was ordered by Colonel von Bothmer (commanding officer of Pr. 67) to occupy the projecting corner of the woods and hold it at all costs. While he was positioning his men in accordance with these orders, he noticed that the Austrian Brigade *Archduke Josef* had deployed about 1,000 paces away behind the Másloved–Chlum sunken road. Before they were more than 50 paces into the woods, the 2nd and 3rd Companies came up against Austrian troops that were only defeated after an intense firefight and were then pursued by both companies. The latter reached the eastern edge of the tall timber and went into position south of the Másloved–Skalka road, thereby establishing contact on the right with the 1st Company. Units of the Austrian IR 51 launched several attacks against them, one after another, but all were repelled. Both companies remained in their designated positions until the end of the fighting for the Swiepwald. After entering the forest, the 4th Company struck off in two directions. Its rifle platoon, under Lieutenant Bömcken, followed those parts of Brigade Poeckh that were falling back to the east (north of the Másloved – Skalka road), while the other two platoons, under *Premier Lieutenant* Freytag, proceeded farther to the left, along the northern border of the woods. At about 100 paces from the edge of the woods, they suddenly came upon a column of the Austrian IR 51 in a thicket. They immediately poured *schnellfeuer* into the Austrians, attacked with the bayonet and drove them off. Similar episodes were repeated many times in many locations, where both opponents ran into each other, oftentimes entirely unexpectedly, and fought furiously.

Advancing further, *Premier Lieutenant* Freytag reached the clearing X west of Hill K and north of the Másloved road, where the company met especially heavy resistance from Austrian *Feldjäger* (presumably belonging the 13th *Feldjäger* Battalion). These were overwhelmed with *schnellfeuer* and *Premier Lieutenant* Freytag (with his two platoons) then proceeded further towards the northeast, where their skirmishers became involved in fighting an advancing Austrian column. The two platoons then fell back towards the north and reached the edge of the tall timber that bounded the sunken meadow E. Not far from there was the 4th Company's rifle platoon (Lieutenant Bömcken), which, constantly skirmishing with the retreating elements of Brigade Poeckh, had reached the edge of the tall timber and there held the projecting angle so that some of its riflemen ended up facing the sunken meadow, while the others faced the northern cleared slope O. On the return march, Lieutenant Bömcken captured Major von Fischer (commander of the 2nd Battalion IR 21) and the few men that remained by his side. Since it was not possible at that time to send them to the rear, he was compelled to take them with him. From the position taken, Lieutenant Bömcken could observe the terrain ahead as far as the Horenoves–Másloved line.

After a brief halt, *Premier Lieutenant* Freytag proceeded towards the southwest and again came to the clearing X. This was now held by Prussian *Jäger* that had become separated from the 2nd and 3rd Companies of the 4th *Jäger* Battalion and who mistakenly fired on Freytag's platoons. Once their error had been explained to them [a euphemism if ever there was one], the *Jäger* placed themselves under Freytag's command. After crossing the Bystrice, the 4th *Jäger* (who had been following the 1st Battalion Pr. 72) marched south as far as the Königgrätz road and at about 11:00 a.m. received orders to advance to the forest. Believing that the Skalka woods and the Swiepwald were connected, the commander of the *Jäger* Battalion, Lieutenant Colonel von Colomb, sent the 4th Company toward the Skalka woods, while the other three companies advanced towards the western edge of the Swiepwald (north of the 4th Company Pr. I/72). [On entering the forest] they initially advanced due east, then gradually swung half right, so that the 2nd and 3rd Companies reached the cleared area north of the Másloved road O, where they became involved in heavy fighting with the remnants of the first wave of Brigade Poeckh. The 1st Company on the other hand, advanced further to the south and was only able to gain ground in the cleared area N south of the Másloved road with heavy losses.

The details of the advance of the Prussian 4th *Jäger* Battalion are as follows. The 1st Company advanced to the corner of the woods south of the Másloved road. The 2nd Company advanced to where the road began, a visible opening at the edge of the woods. The 3rd Company advanced to the corner of the woods north of the Másloved road. The 4th Company, depending on circumstances, was to follow on the left flank as reserve. The skirmishers soon reached the edge of the forest with their close order supports following hard on their heels (at this point effective overall command of the battalion ceased). The 1st Company encountered a few Austrians who were falling back from the edge of the woods and then came upon an entire Austrian column which launched an attack. The *Jäger* company quickly deployed and commenced *schnellfeuer*, which although brief, was so fearsome it caused the Austrians to withdraw to the southern cleared area N, where they took cover behind the stacks of cordwood and were able to resume fighting.

The 2nd Company made it to the edge of the tall timber before running into some Austrians who had established themselves on the track. These fell back before the Prussian *Jägers* and took up a new position on the northern cleared area O before being driven off again by *schnellfeuer*. Part of the rifle platoon under Lieutenant Linsingen lost contact with its own company during the advance. As a result it arrived further to the south and there met up with the 1st Company Pr. II/72, which held the southern corner of the woods projecting toward Cistoves.

The 3rd Company was given that part of the forest north of the Másloved road [F–F] as the objective for its attack. As it drew near it was fired on from the edge of the woods, however it drove the Austrian skirmishers back and followed them eastwards into the interior. There, a large number of troops from Brigade Poeckh (who were drifting about in some confusion) fell on the Prussian company from all sides, the left flank in particular. The right and centre on the other hand, continued to advance in the original direction, pushing the weak and exhausted Austrians back before reaching the western edge of the sunken meadow E.

The 4th Company remained in the Skalka woods before following the 3rd Company into the Swiepwald north of the road [F–F], where it positioned itself between the 2nd and 3rd Companies (without coming into contact with either) securing the rear of the battalion.

The involvement of the two fresh battalions of the Prussian 8th Division not only sealed the fate of what remained of the first wave of Brigade Poeckh, but also had a most deleterious effect on the subsequent attacks of Brigades Württemberg and Saffran.

While Brigades Fleischhacker and Poeckh were engaged in their desperate struggle, the battle raged on unabated in the east. The Austrian 1st and 2nd Battalions IR 12 had called a halt to their attacks on the Swiepwald, but they continued to fire on the Prussians that had established themselves in the eastern margin of the woods and the Havranec, thereby preventing a breakout toward Másloved. However, utterly exhausted and seriously weakened by the preceding hours of bloody fighting, these two battalions were no longer in any condition to meet a determined Prussian advance. When it became apparent that the attack of Brigade Poeckh had failed, Lieutenant Field Marshall *Graf* Thun (who was aware of the weakness of the two battalions of IR 12) ordered Brigade Württemberg to prevent the Prussians from debouching from the eastern and northeastern parts of the forest. Accordingly, Major General Württemberg led the three battalions of IR 57 *Mecklenburg* into the low valley between Másloved and Benátek, where the 1st and 2nd Battalions IR 12 were situated.

The regiment formed up for action south of the pheasantry with the 3rd Battalion on the right, the 1st in the centre and the 2nd on the left. At the same time, horse artillery batteries Nrs. 7/II and 8/II, as well as rocket battery Nr. 11/II of the 2nd Corps Reserve Artillery, moved from the hill southeast of Horenoves (Hill R, the *Tummelplatz*) to the northwestern edge of Másloved. Brigade Battery Württemberg Nr. 4/II (which was also on the *Tummelplatz*) positioned itself to the right of the gun line behind IR 57. During the advance toward the woods, the infantry crossed the Benátek–Másloved sunken road and came without loss to a meadow beyond which were planted rows of medium size plum trees. Here they were met with heavy *schnellfeuer* from enemy troops positioned outside the woods. In order to escape from this predicament as quickly as possible, they immediately launched an assault (without prior fire preparation) and charged the nearly invisible enemy (of whom only a few spiked helmets could be seen here and there).

The left flank of the assaulting regiment came into range of the 2nd Battalion Pr. 66 that was south of the Havranec A, and which had in the meantime been reinforced by the 6th Company that had moved up from Hnewcowes. The riflemen of that battalion had a firm hold on Havranec, while the Fusilier Battalion Pr. 67 was posted partly to the north of the Havranec and partly at the eastern border of the central sector B. Their decimating *schnellfeuer* halted the advance of IR 57's left flank and forced it to take cover behind a rise in the ground but the centre and right managed to push their way into the rear of the 2nd Battalion Pr. 66.

Accordingly, the commander of that battalion, Major Wiedner, had the rifle platoon of the 7th Company, under Lieutenant Reitzenstein, reverse its front against what (in the mist [and gun smoke]) had initially been taken for cavalry. As its assault continued, the Austrians ran into the four Prussian platoons that had advanced earlier, the rifle platoons of the 8th, 11th and 4th Companies Pr. 26 (Lieutenants Engholm, Ponnickau and Platten) as well as a second platoon of the 8th Company Pr. II/66 under Lieutenant Rieben. All were defeated in the first shock. Lieutenant Rieben's platoon retired to Benátek and Lieutenant Engholm's to the central sector of the woods (taking flanking fire from stragglers of Brigade Poeckh that were lurking in the woods west of the sunken meadow). *Premier Lieutenant* Ponnickau was seriously wounded in the thigh, and Lieutenant Platten in the back.

In the meantime, Captain Przychowski hurried to Hill S with the 11th and 12th Companies Pr. F/66, joined by the 1st Company Pr. I/66 (Captain Rauchhaupt). From there they opened a devastating *schnellfeuer* on the Austrians, thereby preventing them from entering the sunken meadow. Lieutenant Reitzenstein's platoon also took part in the defensive fire.

Two companies of the left wing of IR 57 boldly advanced towards the projection of the woods M near Másloved. Alone, from its northeastern tip, the 6th and 7th Companies Pr. II/26, under Captain Fritsch, threw themselves on the attackers. The men of the Austrian 57th opened fire with the greatest rapidity that their muzzle-loaders allowed, but they could not endure the *schnellfeuer* of the Prussians and soon had to retreat, leaving behind a large number of dead and wounded. Among the latter was Captain Matuška. However, the Prussians were also forced to relinquish the field since other troops from the 57th hurried from all sides to the aid of their comrades. The Prussians soon regained the shelter of the woods, from where (along with other companies of their own regiment as well as those of Pr. 66) they poured a veritable hail of fire into the Austrian support troops, compelling them to cease pursuit. Thereupon all the divisions of the Austrian regiment, using the makeshift cover of a field boundary, established themselves in front of the woods and opened heavy fire on the occupied margin. Thus, with the assistance of Brigade Battery Nr. 4/II, which had driven up behind the regiment, the enemy was entirely prevented from breaking out of the forest at that point.

This fire, especially that of the battery, drove Captain Przychowski from Hill S back to his former position in the sunken meadow. He then joined with the companies of his own regiment and the 12th Company Pr. F/66 in the battle against those Austrian units which, after bypassing the 2nd Battalion Pr. 26 and the 1st Battalion Pr. 66 that were fighting in the projection of the woods, continually attempted to advance into the sunken meadow. The 1st Company

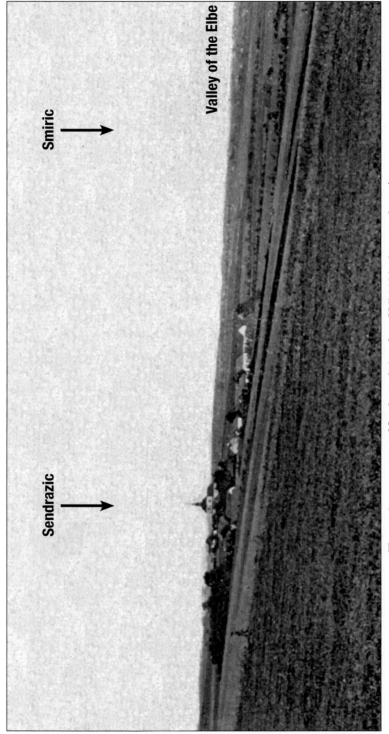

The south-eastern part of Sendrazic (taken from Hill 292 looking south-east)

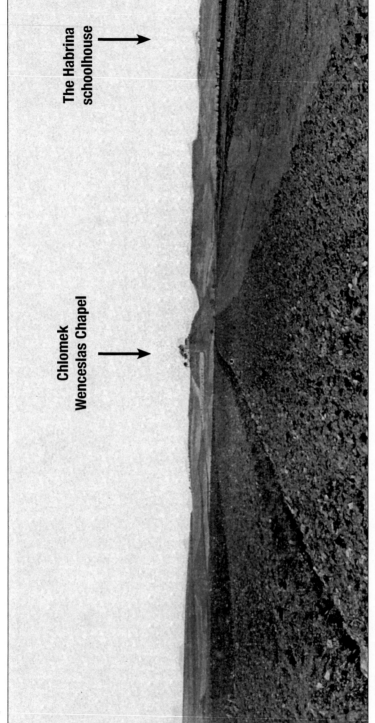

Wenceslas Chapel and Habrina Schoolhouse. Looking west from Hill 263. (Direction of march of the Prussian 12th Infantry Division)

Pr. I/ 66 was ordered back to the southeastern corner of the western sector C, where it was able to view the ground both to the south and to the east, and (to some extent) fire on the advancing Austrians (they could also rake the northern cleared area O particularly well). All the forces on both sides that were fighting in the locations described above remained there until the attacks by Brigades Württemberg and Saffran.

To recapitulate briefly, the events between 10:00 and 11:30 a.m. were as follows. While Brigade Brandenstein was fighting in the forest, the other three brigades of the Austrian 4th Corps deployed for action southwest of Másloved. Of these, Brigades Fleischhacker and Poeckh were ordered to attack the Swiepwald, while Brigade Archduke Josef was designated as reserve. Brigade Fleischhacker advanced toward Cistoves at 10:00 a.m. and captured it. IR 6 *Coronini* then stormed the southern margin of the woods but was repelled by the Prussian *schnellfeuer*. IR 61 then launched several similar attacks also against the southern margin, all resulting in the same lack of success. The brigade then assembled in and around Cistoves and conducted an intense firefight with the Prussians at the edge of the woods and in the two farmsteads west of the village.

In the meantime, the first wave of Brigade Poeckh entered the southeastern corner of the forest. Its left wing defeated all the Prussian units positioned along the southern border and it advanced as far as the western extremity. The centre also advanced and forced the Prussians off the knoll K, while isolated units were able to advance to the northern edge of the woods. The right wing however, took flanking fire from the Prussian companies that were on the ridge, some were even engaged from the rear. The Prussian *schnellfeuer* caused enormous losses. Nevertheless, the right wing stormed the hill and forced the Prussians back but they continued to hold the projection of the woods toward Másloved M. From there, groups of Prussians worked their way behind the first wave of Brigade Poeckh. In addition, two battalions of the Prussian 8th Division hurried to the aid of Fransecky's Division.

This placed the first wave of Brigade Poeckh in an extremely critical situation. The greater part was able to break through and reorganise at Másloved, while the remainder broke up into small, disorientated groups, that milled around in the woods and suffered great losses in constant encounters with the enemy. Only a few of these managed to find a way out and link up with the other elements of the corps. The Prussians remained in possession of the woods. The troops of Brigade Poeckh that were still fighting were essentially trapped and unable to get out.

Section III

Attack of Brigades Württemberg and Saffran. Evacuation of the Woods and Other Events from 11:30 a.m.–3:00 p.m.

Events between 11:30 a.m. and 2:00 p.m.

The desperate situation of Brigade Poeckh (at least that part of it that was still trapped in the woods) prompted Lieutenant Field Marshal Mollinary (at about 11:00 a.m.) to request Major General *Herzog* von Württemberg to disengage his right wing with an offensive advance. However, the major general did not believe that he could immediately comply. He had received definite orders from his own corps commander to remain on the defensive, moreover he also wanted to delay his own attack until the troops of 2nd Corps (that were still to the rear) had come up.

Meanwhile, Lieutenant Field Marshal Thun [2nd Corps] *had* responded to the repeated requests of Lieutenant Field Marshal Mollinary by ordering Brigade Saffran (which had hitherto been holding itself in readiness behind Másloved) to move up, occupy the village and advance in support of Brigade Württemberg. The 11th *Feldjägers* as well as the 2nd Battalion IR 64 *Sachsen-Weimar* passed the village of Másloved. The other battalions of the brigade bypassed the village to the north and having done so, were ordered by the corps commander to attack the woods.

Brigades Württemberg and Saffran, whose battalions had become intermingled as a result of previous fighting, now organised themselves for the attack as follows:

> Right wing: 1st Battalion IR 64 [Saffran] and 1st Battalion IR 80 *Holstein* [Saffran] in the first wave. 2nd Battalion IR 80 [Saffran] and 3rd Battalion IR 80 [Saffran] in the second wave.
>
> Left wing: 11th *Feldjägers* [Saffran] and 20th *Feldjägers* [Württemberg] in the first wave. 1st and 2nd Battalions IR 47 *Hartung* [Württemberg] in the second wave, with the 2nd Battalion IR 64 [Saffran] as support on the hill west of Másloved.
>
> The 3rd Battalion IR 64 [Saffran] held Másloved.
>
> IR 57 *Mecklenburg* [Württemberg] was to remain in position outside the woods. (See Map3).

At this point the situation of the Prussian 7th Division and the two battalions of the 8th Division was as follows [most of 7th Division's formations would have been attrited, some severely].

> In the two farmsteads west of Cistoves 1st Battalion Pr. 27, some of the 2nd Battalion Pr. 27 and the Fusilier Battalion Pr. 27.
>
> North of Cistoves: 7th Company Pr. II/67 and one platoon of the 6th Company Pr. II/27 (the latter under *Premier Lieutenant* Haack, significantly reinforced with stragglers).
>
> At the southern margin of the woods, in the corner opposite Cistoves: 1st Company Pr. I/72 (8th Division).
>
> In Benátek: The half battalion of the 1st Battalion Pr. 26 and the half battalion of the Fusilier Battalion Pr. 26, stragglers from Pr. 27 and a Pioneer company.
>
> In and around the northern sector of the woods, as well as in and around the Havranec: Fusilier Battalions Pr. 66 and 67, 2nd Battalion Pr. 66; and the 1st Company Pr. I/66.
>
> In the projection of the woods toward Másloved M: 6th, 7th and 8th Companies Pr. II/26 and 2nd Company Pr. I/66.
>
> At the projecting angle of the eastern margin of the woods: 5th Company Pr. II/26.
>
> To the southeast T where the Austrian 13th *Feldjägers* had fought: second half of the 1st Battalion Pr. 26 (Horn and Westernhagen), 3rd and 4th Companies Pr. I/66 (Werder) and the half Fusilier Battalion Pr. 26 (Captain Boltenstern).

Those parts of Pr. 26 that had been defeated by Brigade Poeckh (and were able to reorganise themselves and make it to the southern margin, that is in the Austrian rear) joined the 3rd and 4th Companies Pr. I/66, under Captain Werder. The latter two companies originally held the edge of the wooded projection M facing Másloved. They had probably withdrawn from their position and proceeded south only after the attack of Brigade Poeckh (which missed them completely).

The units mentioned below played an extremely important role in the subsequent attack of Brigades Württemberg and Saffran:

> In the open ground between the northern margin of the woods and the village of Benátek: the 2nd, 3rd and 4th Companies Pr. I/67 that had been forced off the ridge by Brigade Poeckh, as well as the 9th Company Pr. F/66 and many scattered groups from all the other regiments of the 7th Division. Of the seven companies of the two battalions of the 8th Division that have not yet been mentioned, six stood along the edge of the tall timber, that is at the track [J–J1, etc.]. South of the road from Másloved [F–F] were the 2nd and 3rd Companies Pr. I/72, the 1st Company and two platoons from the 3rd company 4th *Jägers* (the latter close to the sunken meadow). In the clearing behind Hill K were two platoons of the 4th Company Pr. I/72. The 4th Company, 4th *Jäger* Battalion took no part in the action.

For ease of understanding, it should here be repeated (or as the case may be, added) that the newly reconstituted companies Horn and Westernhagen (formed from the remnants of the 1st Battalion Pr. 26) as well as the half battalion Boltenstern were able to reorganise in the rear of Brigade Poeckh and reach the southern margin of the woods.

The Prussian artillery was still in the same position that it had taken at the start of the battle, with 1⅓ batteries [eight guns] south of Benátek and 1⅔ batteries [ten guns] north of Benátek.

It seems nearly unbelievable that the 5th Company Pr. II/26 (on the eastern face of the projecting angle T) was not only untouched by the attack of the first wave of Brigade Poeckh (directed against the southeastern edge of the woods) but was entirely unaware of it. The sounds of battle coming from the southeast had merely given them the impression that an attack must have been taking place somewhere in that direction. They were engaged with numerous Austrian stragglers that had established themselves in the Másloved–Cistoves sunken road that was about 300 paces from their position. The latter launched frequent attacks but were always repelled by the Prussian's *schnellfeuer*. The Prussian company suffered not inconsiderable losses, especially due to artillery fire, to which it was exposed for the entire time. By 11:00 a.m. it had already lost 50 men. Nevertheless, it bravely held its ground.

At approximately 11:30 a.m. the two brigades, Württemberg and Saffran, began their attack on the woods. A new and bloody struggle was about to commence, which would demand immense sacrifices from both sides. It is most probable that the two (first wave) battalions of the left wing, the 11th and 20th *Feldjäger* Battalions, charged the three Prussian half battalions that were spaced along an 800-pace stretch on the southeastern margin of the woods. They were also supported by the 1st Company Pr. I/72, which was at the corner of the woods facing Cistoves and firing into the left flank of the attackers, as well as large numbers of stragglers who had attached themselves variously.

The history of the Prussian 72nd Infantry Regiment has this to say:

> At about 11.30 am, Lieutenant Linsingen appeared with several men of the 4th *Jäger* Battalion at the position of the 1st Company, and drew Captain Hanstein's attention to the advance of an Austrian brigade toward the southeastern part of the woods. It was the great attack of Brigades Württemberg and Saffran. Captain Hanstein instituted the measures necessary for defence, but the attack took a more northerly direction, and only weak Austrian forces were directed against the company. An enemy battalion appeared at the edge of the southern cleared area but disappeared back into the woods after it came under rifle fire.

Despite their heavy *schnellfeuer*, the three newly formed Prussian half battalions were defeated and retired toward the Hill K, where they continued to resist for some time.

The two battalions of the Austrian IR 47 (second wave, left wing) advanced toward the projection of the woods at Másloved M, but were inundated with *schnellfeuer* from the 6th, 7th and 8th Companies Pr. II/26 and the 2nd Company Pr. I/66 and had to fall back. They renewed their advance and this time reached the edge of the woods where a stubborn hand-to-hand struggle ensued in which the Prussians would have been defeated had they not been reinforced in time by two platoons of the 4th Company Pr. I/72 and two companies of the 4th *Jäger* Battalion. These latter broke forward from their positions in the clearing and the border of the tall timber, and with their help the attackers were again driven back. The Prussians followed the withdrawing Austrians into the open, however they had only gone about 150 paces when they saw the enemy's reserves and thereupon fell back into the woods.

The battalions of IR 47 stormed the forest yet again and this time (even though they were raked at 200 paces with devastating *schnellfeuer*) broke into the woods and drove the enemy

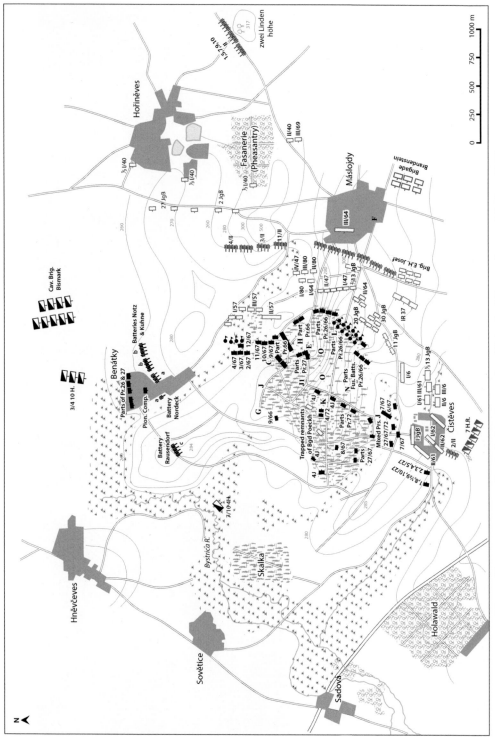

Map 3 The situation immediately before the attacks of Brigades Wurttemberg and Saffran 11:30 a.m.

Northwestern aspect of Nedelist. Taken from Hill 275.

before them. The three companies of the Prussian 26th fell back through the northern cleared area O (pursued by the Austrians) while the *Jägers* and men of Pr. 72nd fell back again into the tall timber.

Led by Lieutenant Colonel von Pistory, the 1st Battalion IR 64 (first wave, right wing) headed for the northern edge of the Másloved projection M, and despite extremely heavy fire, reached their objective with a single charge. The 1st Battalion IR 80 (Major Michele, also first wave) proceeded in a more northerly direction towards the central sector of the woods B and got as far as the sunken meadow, where it came up against such heavy crossfire that its attack failed. During this action Major Michele fell at the head of his battalion. Captain *Graf* Zedwitz assumed command but even as he was in the process of doing so, he fell from his horse, struck dead. The battalion had to give way, with the remnants falling back to Racic where they would again become involved in fresh fighting.

As the Austrian battalions entered the sunken meadow E from the east and from the projection of the woods toward Másloved M, they encountered the following Prussian forces:

> On the slope (of the wave-shaped high ground) that bounded the sunken meadow E to the east: the 11th and 12th Companies 66th IR, under Captain Przychowski.
> In the central wooded sector B: some Fusiliers from Pr. 67 and some of the 2nd Battalion Pr. 66.
> In the western sector C: the 1st and 10th Companies Pr. 66.

As a result of the advance of Brigades Württemberg and Saffran, the 2nd Battalion Pr. 66 (one platoon of whose 8th Company, under Lieutenant Rieben, had earlier been driven all the way to Benátek by the Austrian IR 57) was forced to evacuate its former position south of the Havranec A and fall back into the central wooded sector B. As they were falling back, Captain Diest (8th Company) noticed that an Austrian battalion (presumably the 2nd Battalion IR 57) was following them. Taking a platoon of his own company (to which some of the rifle platoon of the 6th Company, under Lieutenant Boysen, as well as several men of the 5th Company under Lieutenant Ring, had attached themselves) he formed a front facing east along the middle of the eastern edge of the central sector B and opened fire. Although it was believed that the Austrians were several battalions strong, it was only the 2nd Battalion IR 57, whose individual divisions (as was often the case) were probably taken by the Prussians for entire battalions. That battalion came to within 400 paces, halted and returned fire.

Meanwhile, the rest of the 2nd Battalion Pr. 66 had barely made it into [the centre of the] central sector of the woods B when they were ordered to its southernmost point, where several groups Austrian skirmishers had already infiltrated. The rifle platoon of the 7th Company, under Lieutenant Reitzenstein (with skirmishers from the 6th Company still attached to its right wing), advanced 20 paces ahead of the battalion, attacked the Austrians and forced them back. The battalion then established itself at the southeastern point [of the central sector B], with its front facing southeast, alongside some Fusiliers from Pr. 67, and opened fire on the northern cleared area O, where small, isolated groups of Austrians could be seen descending. At the same time, about 600 paces east of the woods, an Austrian battalion appeared from the direction of Másloved, possibly the 4th Battalion IR 47 [the fourth battalions of IR 21, 49, 74 and 47 were assigned to the North Army, see Heidrich's notes on the Austrian Order of Battle later]. The 2nd Battalion Pr. 66 (which was still closed up) wheeled round to face them, while its skirmish line (reinforced by a section from the 26th IR, under Lieutenant Lademann, as well as some Fusiliers from Pr. 67) held the battalion's former front (that is, facing the northern cleared area O). The Prussians (probably the ones that had been defeated earlier by the men of IR 47) fled before the Austrians that were descending the hill, and despite the efforts of Colonel Blankensee, could not be brought to a halt. They broke through their own lines and shaken by the fighting they had endured and the murderous fire of the attacking Austrians, sought shelter in the forest.

Now, closed-up Austrian formations (apparently two battalions strong) began to descend the slope of the cleared area O. The thick swarms of skirmishers that advanced a short distance ahead of them were unshaken by the *schnellfeuer* (of the above-mentioned Prussian skirmish line) and were already within 50 paces when the Prussian skirmishers began to waver. At that moment, perceiving the danger, Major Wieder, the commanding officer of the 2nd Battalion Pr. 66, who had shortly before swung his close order supports to the left, now swung them to the right in support of the riflemen. The Austrian columns, officers to the fore, drove forward resolutely. They were already within a few paces of the 2nd Battalion when the Prussians (for whom the terrain provided the opportunity to form in five tiered ranks, one above the other) opened up with a *schnellfeuer* that thinned the Austrian ranks dreadfully. However, this was not accompanied by lasting success and the Prussian battalion had to fall back behind the central sector B. The 1st and 10th Companies Pr. 66 (who were in the western sector C) also had to fall back. The Prussian reports express their amazement that the Austrian reserves on the hill, and in particular the battalion that was on the flank at that moment, did not enter the fight. The attacking Austrian battalion referred to in the Prussian history must have been the 1st Battalion IR 80, the one on the flank the 4th Battalion IR 47, and the reserve that was visible on the hill the 2nd and 3rd Battalions IR 80.

The five battalions of the Austrian assault column that had entered the woods, and the two battalions of the second wave (the 4th Battalion IR 47 and the 2nd Battalion IR 64) continued to advance irresistibly. The 2nd and 3rd Battalions IR 80 followed on into the projection of the woods facing Másloved M, during which they came under extremely heavy fire from enemy troops at the edge of the tall timber. The commander of the 3rd Battalion IR 80, Lieutenant Colonel Forsthuber, fell here.[1] The Prussians retired on all sides, maintaining a strong *schnell-feuer* as they fell back.

It was a terrible fight. The final climb to the knoll proved especially difficult as it was held by the three enemy half battalions that had been driven from the southeastern margin of the woods (Werder's of the 66th and Horn and Boltenstern's of the 26th). There, in conjunction with the 2nd, 3rd and 4th Companies of Pr. I/72 and the 1st, 2nd and 3rd Companies of the 4th *Jäger* Battalion, they put up a desperate defence. The 1st and 2nd Companies of the 4th *Jägers* defended the southern and northern cleared areas N and O with great determination and launched repeated counterattacks. The centre and left flank of the 3rd Company encountered part of Brigade Württemberg near the western edge of the sunken meadow and were forced

---

1   Ed. Note – In my own copy of the original, the preceding sentence – which I have underlined – has been neatly scored through in pencil. Lieutenant Colonel Forsthuber is also recorded as dying in a separate engagement further on. It is interesting to speculate whether an old soldier, perhaps an eyewitness, made the alteration/correction. I have been unable to determine which account is correct.

back to the track [J–J]. The left wing of the 3rd *Jäger* Company was locked in combat with stragglers from Brigade Poeckh at the northwestern edge of the woods.

As a result of the strong Prussian resistance (which we have outlined above), the Austrian assault columns slowly ground to a halt. Major General Württemberg, whose right wing had already been seriously reduced, found himself obliged to request support from the corps commander, whereupon Lieutenant Field Marshal *Graf* Thun sent forward the remaining available battalions of Brigade Thom. Among these was the 2nd *Feldjäger* Battalion from the Horenoves pheasantry, with its 1st and 2nd divisions positioned behind the right wing of Brigade Württemberg, and the 3rd division behind the three companies of the 27th *Feldjäger* Battalion (Brigade Brandenstein), which had just started to advance (to replace these formations, the 3rd division IR 40 was sent to the pheasantry and the 2nd division to the village of Horenoves to support the 1st division, which was already there). The 2nd Battalion IR 69 moved to support the 1st Battalion of the same regiment in the woods south of Racic.

The two available battalions (the 3rd Battalion IR 69 and the 2nd Battalion IR 40) were being led towards the Swiepwald by Brigadier *Oberst* Thom in person, when it suddenly became evident that major enemy forces were approaching from the north. This was the Prussian 2nd Army commanded by the Crown Prince, which was hurrying to the assistance of the hard-pressed 1st Army and was especially concerned with freeing the 7th Division from its extremely dangerous predicament. To halt the advance of the enemy army, Brigadier Thom was ordered to take position between Másloved and Sendrazic, and (as a matter of the greatest urgency) to cover the withdrawal of [those parts of 2nd Corps that had been committed to the Swiepwald]. Brigade Henriquez, which was positioned in the low ground by the Elbe, was also ordered to proceed to the Sendrazic heights alongside Brigade Thom. Similarly, horse artillery battery Nr. 7/II was moved there from the Hill R, while the other four batteries (Nrs. 1/II, 5/II, 9/II and 10/II) continued the battle that they had already started with the artillery of the Prussian 2nd Army. In the meantime, the battalions of Brigades Württemberg and Saffran continued their attacks in the Swiepwald, soon to be joined by the 30th *Feldjägers* of Brigade Archduke Josef.

Shortly after the entry of the first wave of Brigade Poeckh into the Swiepwald that battalion [the 30th *Feldjägers*] had been moved up closer to the woods from its former position (behind the Másloved–Lípa sunken road) to the Másloved–Cistoves sunken road. From there numerous groups of IR 51 could be seen emerging from the woods, intermingled with Prussians. Soon the space between the battalion and the woods, roughly 400 paces wide, was filled with such groups – a growing number of whom appeared to be enemy. Shortly before the attack of the two brigades of 2nd Corps, Lieutenant Field Marshal Mollinary galloped past the front of the battalion and called out to its commanding officer, Captain von Nemethy, 'The battalion must do well here', and with this exhortation, it formed up for the attack. One company was thrown out from each of the 1st and 2nd divisions as a skirmish line, while the two other companies advanced just behind as supports and the 3rd division followed on as reserve. First the ground ahead was cleared of enemy by several effective volleys, then Captain Nemethy had his bugler blow 'Attack' and the entire battalion advanced towards the forest with a mighty 'Hurrah'. Several groups from IR 51 as well as from the 8th *Feldjägers* attached themselves to the flanks and joined in the assault, storming through the devastating enemy *schnellfeuer* to reach the woods in the in the first charge.

Opposing the 30th *Feldjägers* must have been the 5th Company Pr. II/26 (probably reinforced with stragglers), which had been bypassed and left undisturbed in the earlier attacks.

This company, now reduced to half its complement, fell back northwards [through the forest] to the meadow in front of Benátek, where it later found further employment. At the same time as the above-mentioned *Jäger* attack, the 2nd Battalion IR 64 (designated as support for the first wave) also advanced. After repeated assaults, the Austrian infantry finally succeeded in forcing two of the three Prussian half battalions (those of Captain Werder Pr. 66 and Captain Boltenstern Pr. 26) that were desperately defending the crest of the ridge, down off the high ground, thereby breaking through the enemy Division. Half battalion Werder retired towards the west, and half battalion Boltenstern fell back before the 30th *Feldjägers* towards the north. Half battalion Horn-Westernhagen of the 26th continued to hold its ground in the sector held by the companies of the 72nd and the 4th *Jäger* Battalion at the edge of the tall timber. These latter were primarily threatened by the 2nd Battalion IR 64, which repeatedly attempted to break into their position, however when the Austrians got to within 200 paces they were always driven back by *schnellfeuer*.

The Austrian battalions pursued the Prussians, who for the most part were falling back towards the north and northwest. The lead [companies] of the 30th *Feldjägers* reached the far edge of the woods but were held there by the 5th and 8th Companies Pr. II/26 that had rallied in the meadow under Captain Plötz. Shortly after those companies rallied, many Prussian stragglers appeared at the northern boundary of the woods showing signs of extreme terror and crying out, 'The Austrians are right behind us!' At that very moment, Austrian *Feldjäger* did in fact appear at the edge of the woods and immediately opened fire. It was then that Lieutenant General von Fransecky placed himself at the head of the two consolidated companies and led them against the Austrians. Linking up to right and left with other Prussian units that had rallied in the vicinity, they attacked the *Feldjäger* (who were also being hit in the left flank by the left wing of the 3rd Company of the Prussian 4th *Jäger* Battalion) and drove them back. After a few hundred paces Lieutenant General von Fransecky called a halt and merely pursued the defeated enemy with shooting. *Premier Lieutenant* Gneist, with the 9th Company Pr. F/66, continued to press onwards into the woods and took numerous prisoners, but he soon turned back since the [Austrians] had drawn away from further pursuit by way of a rapid retreat. At the same time, at the western margin of the woods, another group of Austrians were captured bearing the colours of the 3rd Battalion IR 51. This has already been described in the second section of this book.

During the successful action of the Austrian battalions in the interior of the woods, IR 57 was waging a fierce battle in the Havranec. Its orders were to remain in position outside the woods and only support the attack by fire. In the event, however, this proved impossible. At the start of the advance of the other battalions of 2nd Corps toward the forest, the regiment deployed with the 2nd Battalion south of the Havranec A, the 1st Battalion east of it and the 3rd Battalion north of it with front facing west. All three battalions opened heavy fire on the Prussians that were in the central sector B as well as in the meadow between the woods and Benátek. Borne forwards by their eagerness for battle, the 2nd Battalion joined the attack but were met with *schnellfeuer* from the three platoons of the 1st Battalion Pr. 66 (under Captain Diest) that were at the eastern border of the central sector B, and then from the 9th, 10th and 11th Companies of the 67th and had to fall back to their original position with substantial losses.

Shortly thereafter, all three battalions (on their own initiative) launched a joint assault in which the 1st Battalion, under Lieutenant Colonel Görtz, behaved with extreme heroism. This enterprise also foundered in the face of the massed Prussian fire, forcing the brave men of IR 57 back to their previous position with enormous losses, which they did in perfect order. In that assault, the regimental commander, Colonel Gintowd, was seriously wounded in the head by a rifle bullet. Unconscious, he remained where he fell and was taken prisoner.

The principal cause of this failure was that the majority of the Prussians that had been driven from the southeastern margin of the woods, and then from the projection of the woods toward Másloved M, as well as from the northern cleared area O, and had retreated toward the north and emerged from the woods opposite Benátek at the very moment IR 57 launched its attack. These Prussians were quickly rallied on the meadow and joined the fight. It was these, the 6th and 7th Companies Pr. II/26 under Captain Fritsch, the 11th and 12th Companies Pr. F/26 under Captain Boltenstern, and the 11th and 12th Companies Pr. F/66 under Captain Przychowski, that linked up to the left and right of the 12th Company Pr. F/67 that had been fighting there for many hours, and thereby held the stretch from the northwestern corner of the Havranec to the Benátek–Másloved sunken road. Behind them the 2nd, 3rd and 4th Companies Pr. I/67, some of the 2nd Battalion Pr. 66, the 10th Company Pr. F/66, and many of the 27th IR were concentrating.

The lack of success however, totally failed to discourage the brave men of the Austrian 57th. On the contrary, it inflamed their fighting spirit and as the 1st and 2nd divisions of the 2nd *Feldjäger* Battalion advanced toward the northernmost part of the woods it launched yet another assault with the 1st and 3rd Battalions, this time crowned with success because the 1st Battalion was able to push on through the Havranec as far as the eastern margin of the northern tip of the central sector B. The two *Feldjäger* divisions forced the enemy back into the woods and pursued him for a stretch. In the meantime, the 3rd division of the 2nd *Feldjägers* joined with the three companies of the 27th *Feldjägers* that were advancing north of the woods from Horenoves in attacking the village of Benátek. Using the crops as cover, three swarms of skirmishers from the 2nd *Feldjäger* Battalion (led by platoon leaders Macoun and Nitsche, then *Unterjäger* Glaser) reached the entrance to the village and opened brisk fire on some Prussian artillery. After a few minutes, all three swarms fell upon the two Prussian guns that were there, felled the gun crews with rifle butts and bayonets, took hold of one of the guns and dragged it back toward Horenoves. They had already covered a large part of the distance when a platoon of Prussian infantry (commanded by an officer) fell on them to recapture the gun. The *Feldjäger* immediately bayonet charged this new enemy and cut down the Prussian officer and about 20 men, however Prussian reinforcements joined the fight and poured *schnellfeuer* upon them, felling most of the brave *Jägers*. The survivors had to abandon the gun.

By now the advance guard of the 1st Guards Division had already appeared on the right flank of the five *Feldjäger* companies, compelling them to fall back to Horenoves, where shortly thereafter they were joined by the 1st and 2nd divisions of the 2nd *Feldjäger* Battalion. During the retreat, the *Feldjägers* suffered heavy losses from enemy fire. Captain Mudroch, commander of the 1st division, 2nd *Feldjäger* Battalion, fell. Covered by the two divisions of IR 40, the *Feldjägers* gathered in and around the village and then retreated to the linden hill [Hill R]. It was past midday and for the most part the Swiepwald was in Austrian hands.

The situation map of the Austrian General Staff work '*Österreichs Kämpfe im J. 1866*' shows the entire woods as captured by Austrian troops. This representation however, is contradicted by the Prussian side, which describes the situation at midday as follows: 'If one considers the northeastern corners of the villages of Hnevcoves and Chlum to be connected by a straight line cutting through the Swiepwald, then the area of the woods southwest of that line can be considered as untouched by Brigades Saffran and Württemberg.'

However, the Austrians did not have time to celebrate their gains for long. At the very moment they wanted to exploit their victory, to their great astonishment (since only a few knew of the approach of the Prussian Crown Prince's army) they were ordered out of the woods. In order to explain the above statement, we will describe in more detail the approach of those parts of the Prussian 2nd Army that were the immediate cause of the Austrian retreat from the Swiepwald, which they had finally gained after so much struggle.

We know that Lieutenant General von Fransecky had been extremely concerned about his exposed left flank even before the start of the battle. He knew that the advance-guard of the Crown Prince's army was not far from Cerekvic, since on the afternoon of 2nd July Lieutenant von Rundstedt of the Guards Hussar Regiment had arrived in Cerekvic from the 1st Guards Division that was in Doubravic. Guards Colonel von Werder had sent him on a reconnaissance to be briefed on the situation by Colonel von Zychlinski, commander of the Prussian 27th. This of itself failed to provide General Fransecky with the desired reassurance, and so at 3:00 a.m. on the morning of 3rd July, he dispatched *Ordonanz Officier* [*aide de camp*] Lieutenant *Graf* Hohenthal via Bürglitz to establish contact with the advance-guard of the 2nd Army. Lieutenant Hohenthal met up with the advance-guard of the 1st Guards Division at Doubravic, and there learned that the main body of the Division was in Königinhof. Upon his return to Cerekvic, after his report was delivered, he was instructed to immediately ride back to Doubravic and ask the officer commanding there, 'To advance as soon as possible with as many troops as were available and cover the exposed left flank of the 7th Division.' At 8:30 a.m. Lieutenant Hohenthal arrived for the second time in Doubravic, whereupon Major General von Alvensleben issued orders that Colonel von Pape [2nd Foot Guards] was to advance from the village of Liebthal and Colonel von Werder [Guard Fusiliers] from Doubravic, to Jericek. At 9:00 a.m. the two columns moved out and at 11:15 a.m., the advance-guards were united at Zizeloves.

The formation of the advance guard was:

> Commanding: Major General von Alvensleben.
> 2nd Guards Infantry Brigade.
> Column: Colonel von Pape.
> 1st and 2nd Battalions, 2nd Foot Guards Regiment.
> 3rd and 4th Companies of the Guards Jäger Battalion.
> Column: Colonel von Werder.
> 1st and 3rd Battalions, Guards Fusilier Regiment.

Additionally, there were 1st and 4th Squadrons of the Guards Hussar Regiment and two batteries of the Guards Field Artillery Regiment.

As the advance-guard moved out of Zizeloves, Column Werder occupied the villages of Vrchovnic and Zelkovic, while Column Pape marched on toward Benátek. The two batteries drove to the northeast and northwest of Vrchovnic. The first battery had a squadron of Hussars and the 6th Company of the 2nd Foot Guards as escorts, and the second battery had merely a squadron of Hussars (which, in addition, were tasked with establishing contact with the 10th Hussars of Fransecky's Division). South of Zelkovic, Colonel von Pape's column split up and he, along with the 5th, 7th and 8th Companies of the 2nd Foot Guards and the 3rd Company of the Guard *Jägers*, continued on toward Benátek. The remainder (1st Battalion 2nd Foot Guards and the 4th Company Guard *Jägers* under Major Petery) headed toward Horenoves.

In the meantime (12:00 p.m.) the main body of the 1st Guards Division deployed. They had left Königinhof at 7:00 a.m. that morning and marching without knapsacks and with only their field caps reached the road between Chotoborek and Jericek at about 11:00 a.m.. The Guards Heavy Cavalry Brigade also arrived there at the same time and now took the lead. The reserve artillery of the Guards Corps was already south of Jericek, and the combined Cavalry Brigade Bismarck, which formed the extreme left wing of the Prussian 1st Army (covering Fransecky's left flank), linked up with the right wing of the 1st Guards Division. The 5th Squadron of the 2nd Dragoon Regiment [Brigade Bismarck], which was riding ahead, arrived near Horenoves but was forced to turn back by fire from the 3rd Company IR 40 that was posted at the dairy.

Somewhat earlier than the advance-guard of the 1st Guards Division, the Prussian 6th Corps began to exert noticeable pressure on the weak right wing of the Austrian position. It had bivouacked by Gradlitz, the 12th Division moving out at 6:00 a.m., while the 11th moved out at about 7:00 a.m. The former crossed the Elbe at Kukus, advanced via Salney, Westec and Ertina to the Libina Hill (Hill 306) and deployed there at 9:30 a.m. It then marched through Roznov, Neznášov toward Habriná and Chlomek (Wenzel's Chapel). The divisional artillery (two batteries) went into action on the Habrinka Hill (Hill 297), and for a short time fired on the Horenoves Hill. At about 12:30 p.m. the Division then advanced through the woods on the slopes of Horicka Hill toward Racic, where it met up with the 11th Division, which had already occupied the village. Some of the 12th Division crossed (or as the case might be, waded laboriously through) the Trotinka downstream from the village and then joined with the 11th Division to attack the woods south of Racic. The remainder of the 12th Division turned south toward Rodov, crossed the Trotinka [named the 'Trotina' at this point] southwest of that village and then operated against Brigade Henriquez.

After crossing the Elbe at Schurz and Stangendorf, the 11th Division proceeded via Sibojed and Litic to Welchov. It deployed for action between that village and Neujahrsdorf. It then advanced past Hustiran (marching to the sound of guns) towards Racic. Some of the Division crossed the Trotinka north of Racic on the bridge below the confluence of that stream and the Hustiranka, while the rest of the Division waded across further upstream. After 11:00 a.m. the Division deployed for action on the edge of the high ground north of Racic and its four batteries crossed the Trotinka at Luzan. As requested by the 7th Division, they went into position at 11:30 a.m. on the hill north of Racic, supporting that Division by firing on the batteries of the Austrian 2nd Corps on the Horenoves Hill R.

Shortly past noon, the Prussian 21st Brigade broke into Racic, which the survivors of the 1st Battalion IR 80 (after their failed attack on the Swiepwald) had just reached. Three Prussian companies then attempted to advance east of Racic toward the Horenoves Hill, however they were repelled with heavy losses by Austrian shell fire. The brigade then launched an assault on the woods south of Racic, following the two battalions of IR 69 (Brigade Thom) that were withdrawing from there toward Sendrazic.

Already, between 11:30 a.m. and 12:00 p.m., eight batteries of the Prussian 2nd Army had gone into action, two batteries of the Guards at Vrchovnic and Zizeloves, four batteries of the 11th Division north of Racic, and two batteries of the 12th Division on the Habrinka Hill. These fired on the five Austrian batteries on Hill R. Soon after 12:00 p.m., two more batteries of the 1st Guards Division and five batteries of the Guards Reserve Artillery arrived near Vrchovnic. Nine batteries were now present, which in addition to the six batteries of the 6th Corps that were on the left wing, made a total of 90 guns firing on the Horenoves position.

At about 1:00 p.m. the detachment under Major von Petery attacked the village of Horenoves. The commanding officer of the 1st Battalion IR 40, Major Grodecki, was now forced to begin a withdrawal. However, because the evacuation of the village was to be carried out in sequence, one sector at a time, the Prussians were able to encircle them. The 1st division IR I/40 (at the eastern exit of the village) came under heavy fire from swarms of Prussian skirmishers at a range of 250 paces. Lieutenant Philipp of the 1st Company was severely wounded and captured. Thereupon, two platoons of the embattled 1st division deployed and under their protection the rest of the 1st division was able to escape through the houses and towards the hill. Whereupon the skirmish line was recalled. The division had barely made it outside the village, when again it came under flanking fire from two Prussian companies as well as heavy fire from enemy artillery. One shell landed in a tightly packed group of men that had sought shelter behind a fold in the ground. Suddenly the signal 'Cavalry' was sounded. A squadron of the 2nd Brandenburg Dragoons (the 5th) attacked. It rode around the skirmish line and captured the commander of the division, Captain Rabel and *Oberlieutenant* Fritsch. It then attacked that part of the division that was in close order but was driven off by its fire. The squadron rapidly reformed and (on the orders of the commander of the brigade, *Graf* Bismarck, who was present) joined with the 1st Squadron of the same regiment and resumed their pursuit of the retiring division. The division allowed the Dragoons to approach to within 100 paces and forced them to retreat after two effective volleys.

Nevertheless, the Prussians continued their attack against the beleaguered division with fresh forces. Now it was the 1st Squadron of the 3rd Uhlan Regiment (which in the meantime had been attacking isolated skirmishers that were retreating towards the hill) that was sent forward against them. Although it advanced under cover, it was spotted by Bugler Teczar just as it emerged from some dead ground. On his own initiative he blew the signal 'Cavalry', thereby saving the division from catastrophe. His alarm made it possible to form square in time [probably not a true square but a clump with bayonets facing outwards, what the Austrians described as a '*Knaule*'] and repel the attack with well-aimed fire. It went similarly with the 4th Squadron of the Guard Hussars that attacked shortly thereafter. Moreover, its commander was shot from his horse by Platoon Leader Rokyta, who was outside of the square. The division finally reached the heights of Másloved under incessant enemy infantry and artillery fire. There the men threw themselves under the bayonets of the 3rd Battalion IR 64, which had earlier formed square when it was attacked by three squadrons of the 2nd Brandenburg Dragoons.

The 2nd division had started its retreat from Horenoves somewhat later than the first. It was surrounded by the Prussians in a great farmstead that it had chosen to defend, nevertheless it was able to escape through a barn door though with many losses. In so doing Captain Unkelhäuser was severely wounded. On leaving the village the division came under fire from the pheasantry and was threatened by the appearance of enemy cavalry. Despite all this, it reached the high ground with relative ease. In order to avoid arousing the enemy's attention, the colours of the 1st Battalion (that were with this division) were dragged along the ground.

After the capture of Horenoves, the five companies of Petery's detachment pushed on through (and round) the village towards the pheasantry and Hill R.

Since the 3rd division IR 40 (that was posted in the pheasantry had already been recalled to its own brigade at the time when Horenoves was taken by the enemy) and those parts of the 2nd and 27th *Feldjäger* Battalions that had retreated to Horenoves (after the attack on the Swiepwald and Benátek) had continued their retreat, the former to Sendrazic, the latter into *Schanze* 2 [the *Schanze* were field fortifications constructed the previous day, there were six in total], the batteries of 2nd Corps (1/II, 5/II, 7/II, 9/II and 10/II) that were on Hill R, which had fired off nearly all of their ammunition, were in extreme danger and had to be pulled back after 1:00 p.m. They retired via Másloved to the Nedelišt Hill. Major Petery's detachment thereupon took possession of the Horenoves Hill, and the main body of the 1st Guards Division gradually deployed there.

As a result of the reported approach of the Prussian 2nd Army, *Feldzeugmeister* Benedek had his orders sent anew to Lieutenants Field Marshal Mollinary and Thun to retreat to the positions between Chlum and Nedelišt that had been assigned to them in the original disposition. The 4th Corps received this order through Staff Major *Baron* Sacken at approximately 11:45 a.m., and the 2nd Corps just after 12:00 p.m. At 12:15 p.m. Lieutenant Field Marshal Thun ordered 2nd Corps to retreat, which Brigade Saffran began, under the protection of Brigade Thom. Brigade Saffran was to take up position between Másloved and Sendrazic, but the situation was already so unfavourable that it was impossible to carry out the orders as stipulated. Accordingly, Colonel Thom retreated with the forces that were still available to him (the 2nd Battalion IR 40, 3rd division IR I/40 and the 3rd Battalion IR/69) to the hill southwest of Sendrazic and occupied the area around *Schanze* I.

The retreat of the other brigades of 2nd Corps also took place under extremely difficult circumstances. Hardly had the battalions started to move when those parts of the enemy's re-grouped 7th Division went over to the offensive anew, pursuing the Austrian troops and causing them serious losses with rifle fire. Brigade Saffran began its withdrawal about 12:30 p.m. It evacuated the woods at the same time that the Prussian 1st Guards Division seized the *Tummelplatz* (Hill R).

The 11th *Feldjäger* Battalion and the 1st and 2nd Battalions IR 64 fell back to Másloved where they passed through the lines of the 3rd Battalion IR 64 (which was holding the western boundary of the village). The battalion suffered greater losses here than it had during the storming of the woods. Captain von Sursany and *Oberlieutenant* Heinrich, both of the 64th, died heroic deaths. The 11th *Feldjägers* occupied the northern perimeter of Másloved and thereby covered the retreat of Brigade Württemberg.

The 2nd and 3rd Battalions IR 80 (which held the projection of the woods M) assembled several hundred paces from the edge of the forest under enemy fire. However, they were then scattered by the advance-guard of the 1st Guards Division and arrived behind Másloved in a state of complete disorganisation from which they could only be partially restored. The commanding officer of the 3rd Battalion IR 80, Lieutenant Colonel Forsthuber, fell while leaving the woods [but see footnote 1].

Brigade Württemberg's withdrawal from the Swiepwald took place later than that of Brigade Saffran since Major General *Herzog* von Württemberg considered it necessary to avoid leaving the entire area undefended by the simultaneous retreat of 4th and 2nd Corps. If the Prussian 1st Guards Division had succeeded in its advance from the heights south of Horenoves, the retreat of Brigade Württemberg could easily have [become a rout] due to the long time it had spent in the woods. However, the enemy batteries (which in the meantime had been advanced to the Horenoves heights) came under such heavy fire from the Austrian Batteries Nrs. 8/II and 11/II, and later Battery Nr. 4/II of Brigade Württemberg (all of which were positioned west of Másloved, and which in light of the danger looming from the north had made front towards it) that they were only able to maintain a moderate fire. Therefore, for the time being, the enemy infantry delayed advancing over the Horenoves Hill.

Horenoves Hill with the two lindon trees on the horizon. Hill 317.

Spire of the Church of the Transfiguration (Chlum)

The village of Chlum (taken from the west looking east).

Major General von Württemberg used this momentary respite to shift IR 57 to the Másloved heights and, under its protection, have the other battalions of the brigade withdraw from the woods. However, it could no longer take place without fighting the pursuing Prussians. The 1st Battalion IR 47 positioned itself outside the woods on the Másloved Hill and held off the pursuing Prussians for the time being. The commander of the 1st division IR 47, Captain Topi, who bore responsibility for the difficult task of covering the retreat from the woods, proved energetic and successful in fulfilling his mission. The 20th *Feldjäger* Battalion also did its best to delay the enemy advance. Battery 4/II then rejoined its own brigade and repeatedly went into action during the further retreat. Of the batteries of the 2nd Corps Artillery Reserve that had remained at Másloved to cover the retreat, batteries Nrs. 8/II and 11/II pulled back after the withdrawal of the corps to Nedelišt, where they reunited with batteries Nrs. 1/II, 5/II, 7/II, 9/II and 10/II, which had been forced off of the *Tummelplatz* (Hill R).

While Brigades Saffran and Württemberg were retreating, 4th Corps also withdrew. At that time its four brigades were outside the forest. Only the 30th *Feldjäger* Battalion of Brigade Archduke Josef was still engaged at the northern margin and was holding its position. However, when the order to retreat arrived, the fate of the *Feldjäger* changed. The 1st division (which was furthest forward) suddenly ran into a large enemy formation in close order (roughly a battalion in size), which fired volleys and outflanked the *Feldjägers* with a dense skirmish line. The *Feldjägers* also threw out skirmishers to both flanks and held off the Prussians with calm, disciplined fire. When the [Austrian] infantry that had been fighting to their left fell back however, the *Feldjäger* division had to conform. It occupied another position but this resulted in a gap between it and the other two divisions which the enemy was quick to exploit. Under pressure from all sides and cut off from the battalion, the 1st division then had to carry on retreating towards Másloved. Initially it fell back to the point from where the battalion had launched its attack, but it then had to fall back towards Nedelišt, where it finally and permanently lost all contact with the rest of the battalion.

In the meantime, although threatened by significantly superior forces, the 2nd and 3rd divisions continued to stand fast, unshaken. Totally isolated, they repelled the enemy assaults and fought on after all the adjoining troops had started to retreat. They did this for the honour of their name since victory was now out of the question. Suddenly they came under attack from superior forces on two sides, which forced them to commence a fighting withdrawal. During that time, the 3rd division made repeated bayonet charges, thereby disengaging the 2nd division which had lost more than half its men and all its officers save for a single lieutenant. As a result of the firefight that had gone on for hours, ammunition finally began to run out and to complete the tale of misfortune, the batteries at Másloved poured a hail of shells into the Swiepwald in the honest belief that it had already been evacuated by friendly troops. Despite all of this, the retreat was conducted in perfect order as far as the edge of the woods. Once out of the woods, the two divisions met up with the 1st Battalion IR 47, whose 1st division (Captain Topi) was even then launching an attack against the enemy forces that were attempting to break out (of the forest). The two *Feldjäger* divisions assembled alongside this battalion and again went into action. When Captain Topi sank from his horse wounded, the battalion (which had been under heavy attack from the Prussians) had to fall back. The enemy simultaneously threatened the right flank of the 30th *Feldjäger* who once again turned to their bayonets and drove them back. A pause in the fighting now ensued during which the commander of the battalion, Captain Nemethy, ordered his two *Feldjäger* divisions to follow the rest of the withdrawing infantry.

At this point strong enemy forces again broke out of the woods; however, the battery that was positioned on the northern slope of Chlum Hill (Nr. 10/IV), at the request of captain Nemethy, opened up with such an effective enfilading fire that the enemy scattered and hastily fell back into the forest. The 30th *Feldjäger* Battalion was the last to leave the hotly contested, corpse-strewn ground of the Swiepwald and at about 2:00 p.m. it finally linked up with some troops (the 1st Battalion IR 67) from its own brigade.

When Lieutenant Field Marshal Mollinary ordered 4th Corps to retreat, he had the 2nd Battalion IR 68 (Brigade Archduke Josef) occupy the village of Másloved. At this point (between 1:30 p.m. and 2:00 p.m.), the withdrawal of brigades Brandenstein and Poeckh and the corps artillery from the high ground west of Másloved had been completed under the protection of the above-mentioned battalion and the other infantry battalions of Brigade Archduke Josef, which were positioned with front facing north.

However, before 4th Corps had even started its retreat, a fatal incident occurred. Lieutenant Field Marshal Mollinary was riding with his suite from Másloved towards the left wing of the corps when suddenly a volley of about 15 shots was fired from the underbrush at the edge of the woods. The chief of the corps general staff, Colonel von Görtz, fell from his horse, dead. Lieutenant Field Marshal Mollinary's horse was shot from under him, and four more horses were wounded. The 2nd Battalion IR 37 (from Brigade Poeckh) entered the woods at the run but found no enemy there. It appears that at the approach of the horsemen a small party of Prussian skirmishers that were hidden in the woods slipped forward among the great mass of dead and wounded and fired a volley. When the skirmishers of the 2nd Battalion IR 37 drew near, they disappeared back into the forest.

During its retreat from the woods, Brigade Württemberg (as mentioned above) was hotly pursued by the 11th Company Pr. F/66 and the 12th Company Pr. F/77 under Captain Przychowski, the 8th Company Pr. II/66 under Captain Diest, as well as the 6th and 7th Companies Pr. II/26, under Captain Fritschy. These companies pursued the retreating brigade to the place where the Benátek–Másloved sunken road joined the Horenoves–Másloved road. The brigade was also seriously exposed (on its left flank) to Prussian forces that had advanced through the sunken meadow toward Másloved. Aware of the deteriorating situation, General von Württemberg sent a note to Archduke Josef asking him, so far as was possible, to delay the Prussian pursuit. Accordingly, after 1:00 p.m. the 1st and 2nd Battalions IR 37 (to which the remnants of the 8th *Feldjäger* Battalion had attached themselves) briefly went over to the offensive and attacked the woods to the left of Brigade Württemberg. Although this attack failed twice, the brave regiment did not give up and drove the enemy back on the third attempt. However, the latter had already taken up a new position on the next hill and now an extremely stubborn fight developed, during which the enemy received significant reinforcements and was able to renew his advance. The Austrian regiment (which had been greatly depleted in the fighting at Schweinschädel) had become isolated and had to fall back after about half an hour to avoid being cut off by the advance-guard of the Prussian 1st Guards Division that was advancing on Másloved.

The 2nd Battalion IR 37 (which was designated as support) was mistakenly shelled by a friendly battery and was forced (by order of the corps commander) to change position to escape the fire. Therefore, it was unable to cooperate in the above-mentioned attack. After rallying near Másloved, the regiment fell back to the line Nedelišt–Chlum, where in the meantime the other parts of the brigade, as well as Brigade Brandenstein, had arrived.

Brigade Archduke Josef brought up the rear. Its 2nd Battalion IR 68, together with artillery battery Nr. 4/IV, remained in Másloved to cover the brigade's withdrawal. At 2:00 p.m. all three brigades were in their new positions, and only the 4th Brigade, under Major General Fleischhacker, remained in Cistoves since the order to retreat had not reached it.

The batteries of the 4th Corps Artillery Reserve (7/IV, 8/IV, 9/IV, 10/IV and 11/IV) withdrew to Chlum Hill. Battery Nr. 5/IV covered the retreat of the other batteries and only fell back when the troops of 2nd and 4th Corps had pulled back from the high ground around Másloved and the forces of the Prussian 2nd Army had already started to concentrate there. The activity of the latter battery will be described later.

Let us now examine the events concerning the Prussian 7th Division (and the attached battalions of the 8th Division) from the moment the Austrian forces occupying the woods began to retreat.

Battered and exhausted, the Prussians that had been thrown out of the woods stood on the meadow around Benátek. Not until Fransecky's call 'The Crown Prince is coming!' rang out did they start to regain their courage. This call was electrifying. The approach of the army of the Crown Prince was initially confirmed by a change in the direction of fire from the Austrian batteries positioned at the *Tummelplatz*. At 12:45 p.m. the joyful cry 'The Crown Prince is here!' burst forth and with that the awesome mass of artillery near Horenoves and Másloved, which had for so long shelled the Prussians with exact precision, began (though only gradually) to change its deployment and form another front against the new enemy. The stubborn resistance put up by the retreating Austrians also began to slacken. The Prussians arrived from all sides, often setting off in pursuit of the Austrians only to come up against other Prussians.

At this stage the principal Prussian objective was the projection of the woods towards Másloved M and the adjoining high ground. In addition to the individual, isolated elements of Pr. 66, the 9th, 10th and 11th Companies Pr. F/67 and the 3rd Company of the 4th *Jäger* Battalion moved in this direction from the north. In heavy fighting, the 4th *Jägers* made it to the sunken meadow as they pursued the retreating Austrians. There however, they came under extremely heavy artillery fire and were forced to seek cover on the northern slope until other friendly forces caught up. The 1st and 2nd Companies of the 4th *Jäger* Battalion as well as the 4th Company Pr. I/72 came from the west from the tall timber. The commander of the 1st Company, 4th *Jäger* Battalion, *Premier Lieutenant* Schmidt, fell there. At almost the same moment, the above forces succeeded in storming the wooded projection M (that was stubbornly defended by Austrian stragglers), thus cutting off the retreat of those Austrians that were still in the woods. While carrying out this attack, the men of the 1st Company 4th *Jägers* that had pushed forward (along with a half platoon of the 10th Company Pr. F/66) came up against a group of approximately 200 Austrians. They opened up with *schnellfeuer* and the Austrians, with no other way out, were forced to surrender (together with the severely wounded Colonel Weyracher of IR 47). The Prussian account maintains that all the prisoners belonged to IR 47 but that cannot be entirely correct since that regiment lost no more than nine men as unwounded prisoners.

The 4th Company Pr. 72 took part in the affair as follows. As already mentioned, during the attack of Brigades Württemberg and Saffran, *Premier Lieutenant* Freytag and two platoons of his company (the 4th) were in a clearing X where there were also stragglers from the Prussian 4th *Jäger* Battalion. When the battalions of Brigades Württemberg and Saffran retreated, Freytag and his two platoons resumed their advance along the track [F–F] towards Másloved, thereby coming to the southern cleared area N where they were reunited with the 1st Company of the 4th *Jäger* Battalion that had become separated in the fighting. When they reached the cleared area, Freytag's platoons came under heavy fire from which they were only freed by the advancing 3rd Company, 4th *Jäger* Battalion, which hit the firing Austrians in the left flank.

It was 1:00 p.m. when the Austrians finally withdrew from the cleared area. After that time there were no longer any Austrian troops capable of resistance in the adjoining southern parts of the wood, however there were still isolated pockets in the east and the southeast.

There is more to be said regarding the rifle platoon of the 1st Company Pr. I/72 under Lieutenant Bömcken (that you may remember, captured the Austrian Major Fischer and his adjutant). During the attacks of Brigades Württemberg and Saffran, this platoon was at the edge of the tall timber that bordered the sunken meadow E on the west. Since Lieutenant Bömcken considered it was in danger there, he resolved to fall back to the same clearing to which *Premier Lieutenant* Freytag and his two platoons had retreated. However, Lieutenant Bömcken and part of his platoon (with its prisoners) had hardly started their withdrawal when they were surrounded by a group of stragglers from the Austrian IR 51 who were carrying the colours of the 2nd Battalion. The Austrian prisoners regained their freedom while Lieutenant Bömcken and his people now became their captives, and Major Fischer assumed command. Completely disorientated, the little group set off in a direction entirely opposite to the (correct) line of retreat and arrived in the clearing where the other two platoons of the 4th Company, under *Premier Lieutenant* Freytag, had assembled. Here the roles were reversed again and those who had just been freed once more became captive. At this point (as noted earlier) the colours of the 51st were lost. During the retreat of the Austrian Brigades Württemberg and Saffran, Bömcken's rifle platoon joined with the 9th Company Pr. F/66 (*Premier Lieutenant* Gneist) and accompanied them to its former position in the sunken meadow without meeting Austrian troops capable of resistance.

The Prussian forces that had advanced to the eastern edge of the woods facing Másloved took up the following positions. The 3rd Company 4th *Jägers* (under Captain Jännicke) were east of the projection M on either side of the road leading from Másloved to the northwest. To its right and thence as far as the southeastern point of the wooded projection was the 2nd Battalion Pr. 66 (Major Wiedner) with the 2nd Company 4th *Jägers* to its rear. South of the entrance to the spine road [F–F] were the 9th, 10th, and 11th Companies Pr. F/67 under Captain Liebeneiner. These forces, to which groups of stragglers (large and small) had attached themselves, initially fired on the Austrians that were falling back toward Másloved.

Soon thereafter, the Austrian IR 37 launched the attack described earlier (attributed by the Prussians to Brigade Thom). The Prussians were then heavily shelled by a battery positioned northwest of Másloved and it would have gone badly for them by their own estimation if that battery had not been forced to pull back by the advance-guard of the Guards Corps. This courageous battery (Nr. 5/IV of the 4th Corps Artillery Reserve, under Captain Ludwig), which as mentioned above had to cover the retreat of the other batteries of the corps, fell back in bounds to the line Máslowed–Chlum. When it was in one such position on the far side of the Máslowed–Chlum sunken road, men from the Prussian 26th (which had assembled in the southeastern corner of the woods) observed that the battery was without [infantry] cover. When Major Wiedner was informed of this, he cautiously moved towards the battery with his own men (the 2nd Battalion Pr. 66) and the 3rd Company 4th *Jägers* Battalion (together with assorted stragglers). The battery allowed the attackers to come quite close and then raked them with cannister, forcing them to abandon their attempt on the guns and flee back to the protection of the forest. The battery, whose *Oberlieutenant* de Joux was mortally wounded, fired off its entire stock of 63 cannister rounds and then fell back via Chlum.

Prussian accounts state that the 2nd Battalion Pr. 66 was forced to desist from further attacks and fall back to the edge of the woods by [the Austrian guns] and the simultaneous appearance of a column of cavalry from the south. This cavalry must have been the Austrian 7th Hussars, which in the afternoon took post east of Cistoves and thus could have been seen there by the Prussian forces emerging from the woods.

We must still deal with the events around Cistoves itself, which we left earlier just after 11:00 a.m. At this time, in and about the orchard way north of the village were: the 7th Company Pr. II/67 (under Lieutenant Vorberg), to their left the platoon of *Premier Lieutenant* Haack (significantly reinforced with stragglers) and to its right more stragglers from the 27th. To the east of these forces, with front facing east and southeast, were two platoons each of the 1st and 6th Companies Pr. 67. The two isolated farmsteads west of Cistoves were held by the 1st Battalion Pr. I/27, the 5th Company Pr. II/27 and the remnants of the 9th Company Pr. F/27.

The defenders of Cistoves did not let themselves be discouraged by the failed attack against the southern border of the Swiepwald. On the contrary, they kept the Prussians on their toes with repeated, powerful assaults. Austrian *Feldjägers* of the 1st Battalion had established themselves in the barns and houses on the eastern boundary of Cistoves, as well as outside the village in the sunken roads and behind the slightest fold or rise in the ground. From these positions they kept up constant, well-aimed fire on the enemy, while the infantry that was in the village directed their attack, in part from the northeastern corner of the village against *Premier Lieutenant* Haack's platoon, and in part from the main entrance to the village and thus more against the stragglers from the 27th that were on the right flank of the 7th Company Pr. II/67.

It seems to have been primarily *Feldjägers* that attacked the 7th Company Pr. II/67 (at least that is what follows from the regimental history), in which a sortie by two columns of the 1st *Feldjägers* is described, and which is said to have met with a column of the 1st Company Pr. I/67 under Lieutenant Schneider that had advanced from the east and opened up on the *Feldjäger* with *schnellfeuer*, forcing them to fall back. The Prussians followed hard on the heels of the withdrawing Austrians as far as the edge of the village and took many prisoners. The *Feldjäger* that had advanced from the west came up against the 7th Company Pr. II/67, which poured *schnellfeuer* into them even while they were still in the sunken road. Despite heavy losses, the *Feldjäger* still pressed forward to within 40 paces of the Prussians before they too were finally forced to fall back.

Lieutenant Vorberg pursued the *Feldjäger* with a part of his company, took many prisoners and was fortunate enough to capture a barn where he happened to find 20 *Jägers* (most of them wounded in the head or neck), but despite all his efforts he was unable to take the next objective. He therefore requested support from Captain Müller of the 6th Company, who was unable to accede to this request because he had to repel assaults on his own left flank. These and similar isolated actions continued, and it was only as a result of the success of the attacks of Brigades Württemberg and Saffran (whose repercussions were felt even here) that the Prussians (by their own account) were forced to fall back to the southern margin of the woods.

Lieutenant Vorberg's company (7th Company Pr. II/67) met Lieutenant Linsingen's platoon of the 4th *Jägers* at the edge of the woods, as well as Company Hanstein (4th Company Pr. I/72). Lieutenant Vorberg's company took position alongside these, while *Premier Lieutenant*

Haack and his platoon, along with the assembled stragglers of its own regiment, turned toward Benátek, arriving there at 1:30 p.m.

The history of the Prussian 27th IR describes the courage of the Austrian troops that held Cistoves:

> Heedless of losses the attacks continued. ... Here one saw officers out in front of their men, swinging their sabres. Here too, the columns advanced with drums and 'Hurrahs' to extremely short range, at times only 30 paces, but they were always driven back by the *schnellfeuer* that produced a truly gruesome slaughter. *Premier Lieutenant* Haack stated that in order to maximise the effect of their fire, in what was for them a desperately critical moment, his men finally held their rifles horizontally at the hip, loading and firing so that they would rarely miss their easy target. Repeatedly the heat of the barrels made it hard to hold the rifles. Thus, the hail of fire smashed into the tightly packed ranks of the assaulting enemy, causing fearful losses.

Of the two isolated farmsteads, the one closest to Cistoves was held by the 2nd, 3rd, and 4th, as well as the remnants of the 5th, Companies of the Prussian 27th, which immediately set to work to preparing it for defence. The rifle platoons of the 2nd and 3rd Companies worked their way forward towards Cistoves, taking cover in the hollows and ditches close to the western boundary of the village, from where they opened a steady fire on the Austrians in the buildings. This went on for several hours until Captain Schöler launched a platoon attack against the edge of the village, but it was bloodily repelled.

Somewhat later, Captain von Werder advanced with a platoon against some buildings that jutted out to the northwest. He succeeded in capturing a barn, from which his platoon was then gradually able to work its way ever deeper into the village, from farmstead to farmstead, until finally it reached the crossroad, though with many losses. 'For the Austrian *Feldjäger* well knew how to hit their targets from behind cover,' says the regimental history of the Prussian 27th.

Even though the situation was not as desperate for the Prussians in these isolated farmsteads as it had recently been, nevertheless all eyes were turned to the east, from which help was eagerly awaited. In the western farmstead (in which a little old woman remained, working tirelessly and zealously to help the numerous wounded who had been gathered there) measures were also taken to prepare it for defence since an Austrian attack could be expected soon. Towards Cistoves, a skirmish line had established itself in a ditch. Those in the farmsteads suffered less from rifle fire than from artillery, the battery at Lípa sent over a few rounds from time to time, its shells exploding in the narrow barnyards.

By now the defenders had been anxiously watching the surrounding fields for almost three and a half hours, but there was no sign of an impending release from their difficult situation. By 2:30 p.m. there was still nothing to suggest a Prussian victory was in the offing, the burden of doubt grew heavier, their concern ever deeper. At last, however, the rumble of gunfire could be heard from the east and it became evident that several Austrian batteries at Másloved were changing front. Finally, the anxious defenders were surprised by a convincing 'Hurrah' that came from Cistoves and by the retreat of Brigade Fleischhacker.

The hard-pressed men of the 27th were relieved by three companies of the 2nd Battalion, Guards Fusilier Regiment (part of the advance-guard under Major General von Alvensleben) that advanced from Másloved and pushed into Cistoves. While the Guard Fusiliers pursued the retreating Austrians, those of the 27th that were fighting near Cistoves were organised by Colonel Zychlinski into an *ad hoc* battalion that General von Gordon later led towards Langenhof.

The retreat of Brigade Fleischhacker took place under the most unfavourable circumstances imaginable. As the three brigades of his corps began to retreat from their position at Másloved, Lieutenant Field Marshall Mollinary sent orders (with an officer) to Brigadier Fleischhacker, commanding him to withdraw also. However, this order did not reach Fleischhacker, and since he was unaware of the changes that had taken place on the right wing of the Austrian army [the arrival of the Prussian 2nd Army], he and his brigade remained in position at Cistoves. Worse still, when he finally resolved to leave, he issued orders for a retreat to Nedelišt via Chlum (the battery was to go via Másloved) without realising that Chlum and Másloved had already been captured by the Prussians. Thus, the way was already blocked in both directions.

During the advance of the main body of the 1st Guards Division from Másloved towards Chlum, by order of the divisional commander, the advance-guard under Major General von Alvensleben dropped back to cover the right flank. The 1st and 2nd Battalions of the Guards Fusilier Regiment, the 2nd Battalion of the 2nd Guards Regiment and the 3rd Company of the Guards *Jäger* (Colonel von Pape) were to take position in the hollow northeast of Másloved. Major Petery's detachment with the 1st Battalion of the 2nd Guards Regiment and the 4th Company of the Guard *Jägers* was ordered to position themselves on the strip of meadow between Másloved and the village of Chlum. Colonel von Pape's column followed the main body in echelon (behind its right wing) and at 2:30 p.m. reached the meadow between the two roads that ran from Másloved towards Chlum. At the same time, the men of Brigade Fleischhacker began to evacuate their position in and around Cistoves. However, the Prussian columns referred to above scuttled the planned Austrian retreat. The battery, after a heroic struggle, fell into enemy hands. The 7th Hussars, after a wild cross-country pursuit, were more than decimated before they reached Nedelišt. The infantry ran into the main body of the Prussian advance-guard and was simultaneously taken in the front, the left flank and also the rear. For a long time, it was tossed back and forth before finally fighting its way through, but at enormous loss. The breakthrough took place under extremely heavy enemy fire, in part between Lípa and Chlum, in part through Chlum itself.

Reassured by the general advance of the Guards, at about 1:30 p.m. Lieutenant General von Fransecky ordered the 7th Division to assemble on the meadow between Benátek and the northern tip of the woods. According to consistent accounts from all the Prussian forces that were fighting in the Swiepwald, most of the Division had already carried out this order by 2:00 p.m. and at 3:00 p.m. the [severely depleted] Division marched off to Chlum via Másloved.

By order of Lieutenant General von Fransecky, the 1st Battalion Pr. 72 remained in the Swiepwald to recover the wounded, a great number of whom lay in the interior. The few houses in Benátek that were not in ruins were hastily prepared for their reception. The battalion performed this Samaritan work for an hour. In this relatively short time, something between 1,000 and 1,500 wounded were carried out of the woods and placed at the projecting angle east of the road to Benátek. The magnitude of the sacrifice that the battle in the Swiepwald exacted can be seen by the fact that the wounded collected by the battalion comprised less than half of the wounded that were present in the southern part of the woods alone. How many of them must have lain helpless for hours in the other parts! More than 4,000 dead and approximately 7,000 wounded covered the ground in and around the Swiepwald. The Austrian General Staff work is correct when it says: 'One cannot walk upon this field of battle where brave men fell in the most stubborn struggle, without the most profound emotion.'

To summarise briefly the events in the Swiepwald from 11:30 a.m. to 2:00 p.m. In order to free those parts of Brigade Poeckh that remained in the forest, as well as to finally gain complete possession of it, at 11:30 a.m. two brigades of the 2nd Corps (Brigades Württemberg and Saffran) were sent into the attack. After many attempts and great losses, the Prussians were driven from the greater part of the woods. At the very moment when the Austrian battalions achieved success, the Prussian 2nd Army (under the Crown Prince) appeared on their right flank. As a result the two Austrian brigades were ordered to retreat from the woods and proceed to the line Chlum–Nedelist. This withdrawal was carried out with constant fighting and substantial losses. Nevertheless, the men of both corps did succeed in reaching their new positions after considerable effort.

Throughout the entire time, extremely bloody fighting continued between the Austrian troops in Cistoves and parts of the Prussian 27th and 67th infantry regiments, with the latter vainly attempting to take Cistoves and oust Brigade Fleischhacker. That brigade did not consider retreat until the advance-guard of the Prussian Guards Corps approached Cistoves with superior forces, leaving it with no alternative but to break through towards Königgrätz.

Organisation of the Austrian and Prussian Armies in the Year 1866

The Armed Forces of Imperial Austria

The Infantry

The infantry was organised into 80 line regiments, 14 border [Grenz] regiments and one border infantry battalion.[1] Each line infantry regiment had three field battalions, consisting of six field companies each. Two field companies formed a division. Each line infantry regiment also included an independent fourth battalion which also consisted of six companies. Each replacement district command [Ergänzungs Bezirks Commando] of the 80 line infantry regiments retained a depot division, which in peacetime remained *en cadre*. The line infantry regiment of three field battalions had a wartime strength of 81 officers, 3,226 men, 89 horses and 26 horse-drawn vehicles.

In total, 56 of the line infantry regiments were with the North Army and 23 with the South Army. One was with the German Federation Army [Deutsche Bundesarmee] (VIII Corps, Brigade Major General Hahn).

The 240 field battalions of the line infantry regiments were assigned as follows:

With the North Army, in brigade formations	164
With the South Army, in brigade formations	68
With the German Federation Army	6
Total	240

1   Tr. Note – Archduke Ferdinand I, younger brother of Emperor Charles V of Spain, and afterwards Charles V, Holy Roman Emperor, solved the problem of defence of his southeastern frontiers through a system of fortifications and military colonies. Small groups of mercenaries garrisoned a crude but effective chain of fortifications along the Hungarian border. He settled Christian Balkan refugees in a network of fortified villages, watchtowers and blockhouses protecting the Croatian Uplands. In return for military service, he granted these colonists substantial privileges. These colonies, in time, became a significant military force. The *Militärgrenze* thus became a permanent part of the Habsburg military system. In 1851 the Transylvanian *Grenz* regiments were dissolved as unreliable, leaving the regiments of Croatia–Slavonia and the Banat of Temesvár. These remaining *Grenzer* regiments were mobilised for the Austro-Prussian War in February 1866. (Gunther Erich Rothenberg, *The Army of Francis Josef* (West Lafayette, IN: Purdue University Press, 1976), pp. 2, 43, 61 and 67)

The fourth battalions of the 80 line infantry regiments were assigned as follows:

The fortresses of Krakau 10, Olmütz 10, Theresienstadt 7, Josefstadt 5, Königgrätz 3	35
As fortress garrisons in Italy	17
As staff troops with the North Army (from IR 4, 8, 16, 27, 79, 80)	6
With the North Army in brigade formations (from IR 21, 47, 49, 55, 56, 58, 71, 74)	8
With the South Army in brigade formations (from IR 7, 17, 22, 59, 76)	5
In Istria, (from IR 15, 65, 66, 70, 77)	5
In Dalmatia (from IR 3, 69)	2
In the Tyrol (from IR 14)	1
Total	80

Therefore, in North Army there were 164 field battalions and eight fourth battalions – a total of 172 battalions in brigade formations. Infantry Regiments 58 and 71 had all four battalions in one and the same brigade. The fourth battalions of Infantry Regiments 55 and 56 were assigned to Brigade Procházka of 3rd Corps. The fourth battalions of Infantry Regiments 21, 49, 74 and 47 were assigned to the North Army because the third battalions of the first three regiments were with Brigade Hahn of the German Federal Army, while the third battalion of the last-named regiment remained behind as garrison in Dalmatia.

Seven of the line regiments were brought up to full strength in Venetia: Nrs. 13, 16, 26, 38, 45, 79 and 80.

In order to increase the armed forces for what was to be a war on two fronts, a variety of measures were instituted, none of which could be carried out fully or prove their worth because events in the northern theatre of the war influenced the ongoing organisation. In May 1866, the existing depot divisions were placed on a wartime footing, and as well as the depot division of each of the 80 line infantry divisions, a second depot division was activated. These two divisions (four companies) were then combined to form a fifth battalion (of four companies). These fifth battalions were considered replacements for the fourth battalions as garrison troops when the fourth battalions were turned over to the field army. In the event, this measure provided two *Grenz* infantry regiments and ten battalions of line infantry that were then employed with the field army. However, since the second depot divisions of the Bohemian and Moravian (as well as several Galician and Hungarian) regiments were transferred, respectively, from Bohemia or Galicia to Hungary and Italy, and then from Hungary and Galicia to Vienna, the activation of the fifth battalions only took place for 33 infantry regiments: for the seven Venetian regiments and then for regiments Nrs. 2, 31, 50, 51, 62, 63, 64, 9, 15, 24, 55, 58, 41, 5, 12, 19, 44, 48, 52, 65, 66, 67, 70, 71, 72 and 76.

However, these battalions did not exist for long, for on 23 June the formation of ten combined battalions Nrs. 1–10 took place by consolidating 30 second divisions, and since 11 divisions were taken from the above-mentioned fifth battalions, only 22 fifth battalions remained. The second depot divisions of the following regiments were employed in activating the above formations: Nrs. 1, 4, 8, 27, 47, 49, 20, 56, 57, 9, 15, 55, 24, 58, 65, 5, 39, 66, 33, 37, 68, 44, 46, 52, 19, 32, 69, 25, 34 and 60. This was followed immediately by the order to activate an additional ten combined battalions Nrs. 11–20, which were to be formed from the second depot divisions that had been relocated in Hungary and Siebenbürgen [Transylvania]. The latter belonged to the following regiments: Nrs. 35, 42, 73, 28, 36, 74, 18, 21, 54, 3, 12, 71, 48, 72, 76, 40, 67, 70, 10, 30, 77, 6, 53, 78, 23, 29, 43, 50, 61 and 64.

Since this measure resulted in the disbanding of nine of the still extant 22 fifth battalions, only 13 now were left: seven of the fifth battalions of the Venetian regiments – Nrs. 13, 16, 26, 38, 45, 79 and 80 – and Nrs. 2, 31, 41, 51, 62 and 63. Of these, six fifth battalions of the Venetian regiments were employed as garrisons in Vienna and one in Linz, as well as one from Nr. 41 in Czernowitz, and the other five regiments formed the garrison in Siebenbürgen. Of the 80 second depot divisions that were activated, 73 (60 + 13) were employed in battalion forma-tions, while of the seven remaining, those of Infantry Regiments Nrs. 11, 14, 59 and 75 were employed with the Operations Army in the Tirol (they formed the Half Brigade Loos) and those of Infantry Regiments Nrs. 7, 17 and 22 were employed as garrison troops in Carinthia and Carniola.

The 20 combined battalions that were formed from the 60 second depot divisions were consolidated into three brigades, one of which (Müller) was with its main body (five battal-ions) stationed at Olmütz, while the other two (Anthoine and Lebzeltern, along with the rest of Brigade Müller) were stationed in Vienna. The last named were committed to garrison the Floridsdorf bridgehead. If needed, these three brigades were to be consolidated as a mobile reserve corps.

As a result of the great losses suffered by the North Army, on 11 July all the combined battalions and all the second depot divisions of the 80 infantry regiments were disbanded and employed to replenish their regiments.

Since, as described above, the projected activation of the fifth battalions from the 1st and 2nd depot divisions was not fully carried out, the first depot divisions of 67 Infantry Regiments remained available and were specially employed. During the mobilisation and at the start of the war, they remained in those provinces where they had been mobilised. Those of the Hungarian regiments were for the most part concentrated in the fortresses of Ofen and Komorn, and those of the Bohemian regiments in Prague. However, after the Battle of Königgrätz the first depot divisions of the Bohemian and Moravian regiments had to be transferred to Hungary because of the enemy invasion.

The infantry was armed with a muzzle-loading percussion rifle and socket bayonet. The rifle bullet had a cylindo-ogive form. The infantryman carried 60 cartridges on his person. In the battalion ammunition wagon and the various ammunition parks were a total of 130 additional rounds for each infantryman or *Jäger*.

Grenz Infantry Regiments

The 14 *Grenz* [border] Infantry Regiments and the independent *Titler Grenz* Infantry Battalion[2] came to full strength in the military border land that existed at that time. Each regiment was organised in peacetime into two battalions of six companies each. In war this was increased to three battalions, also of six companies each. The *Titler* Battalion had the same number of

---

2   Tr. Note – In 1849, in conjunction with the formation of a Danube fleet, the *Tschaikistenbataillon* (originally named from the Turkish work 'Kaik' meaning oared boat) was renamed as the *Titler Grenz Infanteriebataillon*.

companies. In the event of war, Infantry Regiments Nrs. 1, 2, 3, 5, 6, 7, 8, 9, 12, 13 and 14 as well as the *Titler* Battalion each activated a depot division. A *Grenz* regiment on a war footing with three battalions had a complement of 81 officers, 3,049 men, 94 horses and 27 horse-drawn vehicles.

During the 1866 campaign, *Grenz* Infantry Regiments Nrs. 1 and 2 were in Dalmatia, Nrs. 3–12 and the Titler Battalion were with the South Army, Nr. 13 was with the North Army (Brigade Procházka, 3rd Corps) and Nr. 14 was in Siebenbürgen. The depot battalions of Infantry Regiments Nrs. 1 and 3 were employed in Istria, those of Nrs. 6 and 7 in Komorn, Nr. 9 in Arad, Nr. 12 in Temesvár, Nr. 13 in Esseg, Nr. 14 in Peterwardein as garrisons, or as the case may be, occupation troops. The depot division of Infantry Regiment Nr. 2 was in Zeng, that of Nr. 5 in Istria and that of the *Titler* Battalion in Brod-Gradiska. They were armed similarly to those of the line infantry regiments.

Jäger Troops

The *Jäger* troops consisted of the *Kaiser Jäger* Regiment and 32 *Feldjäger* battalions. The *Kaiser Jäger* Regiment consisted of six battalions of six companies each and a depot battalion, which remained *en cadre* in peacetime. Each of the 32 *Feldjäger* battalions consisted of six companies and one depot company, the latter 'en cadre'. A *Jäger* battalion [*Feld* and *Kaiser*] had a wartime complement of 27 officers, 1,080 men, 33 horses and 9 horse-drawn vehicles.

Two of the 32 *Feldjäger* battalions, Nrs. 8 and 26, were brought up to full strength in Venetia.

At the start of May 1866, a second depot company was ordered to be activated for all *Jäger* battalions, and on 29 May, the second depot company of 30 battalions (Nrs. 23 and 28 were excepted) were consolidated into five new battalions, which were designated 'Combined *Jäger* Battalions' and assigned the numbers 33–37. Battalions Nrs. 36 and 37 were concentrated in Verona, and the other three in Vienna.

The battalions were activated as follows:

Nr. 33 from the second depot companies of battalions	Nrs. 1, 13, 2, 14, 6, 18
Nr. 34 from the second depot companies of battalions	Nrs. 17, 25, 31, 5, 4, 16
Nr. 35 from the second depot companies of battalions	Nrs. 8, 26, 12, 22, 24, 30
Nr. 36 from the second depot companies of battalions	Nrs. 29, 32, 7, 19, 20, 27
Nr. 37 from the second depot companies of battalions	Nrs. 3, 15, 9, 10, 11, 21

Eight of the 37 *Feldjäger* battalions, Nrs. 7, 10, 15, 19, 21, 23, 36 and 37, were employed with the South Army; one, Nr. 35, with Brigade Hahn of the German Federation Army; and the remaining 28 with the North Army. Three battalions of the *Kaiser Jäger* Regiment were with the South Army and the other three, as well as the depot battalion, were with the southern forces in the Tirol.

A total of 27 of the 29 infantry brigades of the North Army had *Feldjäger* battalions, while 26 of the brigades had one *Feldjäger* battalion each. Only Brigade Procházka had two: Nrs. 33 and 34. Brigade Wimpffen (10th Corps) and Rothkirch (8th Corps) lacked a *Feldjäger* battalion; however, each regiment of these two brigades had four battalions.

The two depot companies of *Feldjäger* Battalions Nrs. 23 and 28 were consolidated into a depot division, which served as garrison troops in Siebenbürgen. The 1st Depot Company of the other 30 battalions remained (with the exception of those of the two Venetian Battalions Nrs. 8 and 26) in those districts where they had been brought to full strength. The two Venetian depot companies were shifted to the Steiermark.

In the month of June, due to the enemy invasion, the 1st Depot Companies of the Bohemian and Moravian Battalions were transferred to Hungary, where they remained until peace was concluded.

The armament of the *Jäger* troops consisted of a muzzle-loading piece with *Haubajonett* [socket bayonet with a broad blade]. Each *Jäger* carried 80 cartridges. An additional 130 rounds per man were carried in the battalion ammunition wagon and in the various ammunition parks.

Cavalry

The cavalry was organised as heavy [reserve] and light cavalry, and in peacetime consisted of 235 squadrons. The heavy cavalry comprised 12 Cuirassier regiments [Cuirassier in name only, they had divested themselves of their armour in 1862] and the light cavalry comprised two regiments of Dragoons, 14 of Hussars and 13 of Uhlans.

Every Cuirassier regiment consisted of five squadrons in peacetime (with the exception of the 8th, which had six). The regiments of the light cavalry all had six squadrons. In the event of mobilisation, each regiment left one squadron (the depot squadron) behind for replacements. Thus, each regiment went into the field with four, or as the case might be, five squadrons.

A Cuirassier regiment with four squadrons had a wartime complement of 26 officers, 704 men, 651 horses and 12 horse-drawn vehicles. All the other cavalry regiments had a complement of 32 officers, 878 men and 812 horses. All 12 Cuirassier regiments were consolidated during the 1866 campaign into six cavalry brigades, and these into three Cavalry Divisions. An Uhlan regiment was attached to each of the six Cuirassier brigades. The other cavalry regiments were in part consolidated into brigades, or as the case might be, into Divisions, and some were attached to the army corps. In 1866 all the Cuirassier and Dragoon regiments as well as ten Uhlan and ten Hussar regiments were with the North Army, four Hussar and two Uhlan regiments were with the South Army and one Uhlan regiment was in Krakau.

The requisite staff cavalry, which amounted to 4½ squadrons in the North Army, was taken from the field squadrons of all the cavalry regiments, as was the cavalry assigned to the fortresses. Two squadrons were in Olmütz, one in Theresienstadt, ¾ of a squadron in Josefstadt and ¼ of a squadron in Königgrätz, giving a total of four squadrons employed as fortress cavalry.

The depot squadrons of ten Hussar regiments were in Carinthia and the Steiermark, and four more Hussar regiments and one Uhlan regiment were in Galicia. The depot squadrons of the other Uhlan regiments and all the depot squadrons of the Cuirassier and Dragoon regiments were in Hungary.

The Uhlans were armed with lance, sabre and pistol. The other cavalry was armed with sabre and pistol, and 20 men of each squadron were also armed with carbines. Each cavalryman carried 24 rounds [in Edelsheim's 1st Light Cavalry Division all the troopers were armed with the carbine].

Field Artillery

The field artillery consisted of 12 regiments with a total of 133 batteries. Each of Field Artillery Regiments Nrs. 1, 2, 3, 4, 5, 7, 8, 9 and 10 had 11 batteries each, six 4-pounder foot batteries (Nrs. 1–6), two 4-pounder horse artillery batteries (Nr. 7 and 8), two 8-pounder foot batteries (Nr. 9 and 10) and one rocket battery (Nr. 11). In peacetime, two of the 4-pounder foot batteries had only four guns [as opposed to the normal eight], each with teams of horses. The other eight gun batteries had eight guns each with teams. Artillery regiments Nrs. 6, 11 and 12 had ten batteries each: one 4-pounder foot battery, five 4-pounder horse artillery batteries and four 8-pounder foot batteries. In peacetime one 4-pounder foot battery and one horse artillery battery had four guns provided with teams of horses, while the other eight batteries had eight guns with teams. In peacetime regiment Nr. 5 had two 3-pounder mountain batteries. In the event of mobilization, two additional batteries were added.

In the event of war, the 133 available batteries had fifty-seven 4-pounder foot batteries, thirty-three 4-pounder horse batteries, thirty 8-pounder foot batteries, nine rocket batteries and four 3-pounder mountain batteries, all consisting of eight pieces.

In the 1866 campaign these were assigned as follows:

Batteries with the North Army	92
Batteries with the South Army, including the four mountain batteries	28
Batteries in the northern fortresses	5
Battery in the Venetian fortresses	1
Batteries in Istria	4
Batteries with Infantry Brigade Hahn of the German Federation Army	2
Batteries with the combined Infantry Brigade Müller	1
Total batteries	133

Over and above these, at the end of June 1866, activation was ordered for an additional twelve 8-pounder and four 4-pounder foot batteries, which were designated for the Armies of the North and South, as well as for the newly activated combined infantry brigades.

The wartime complements were as follows:

4-pdr foot battery	4 officers	159 men	109 horses	21 train wagons
4-pdr horse battery	4 officers	180 men	147 horses	22 train wagons
8-pdr foot battery	4 officers	192 men	147 horses	22 train wagons
Rocket battery	3 officers	120 men	61 horses	12 train wagons
3-pdr mountain battery	2 officers	103 men	2 horses	61 pack animals

The rocket batteries were equipped with 4-pound *Schussraketen* [flat trajectory rockets] and 6-pound *Wurfraketen* [high trajectory rockets]. Additionally, they fired *Buchsenkartatschen*, [a fixed, short range anti-personnel rocket similar to shrapnel] *Brandballen* [an incendiary rocket] and *Leuchtballen* [an illuminative rocket]. The first was used up to a range of 2,000 paces, the second to 1,500 paces, the third to 300 paces and the last two up to 1,000 paces. [The standard load for a rocket battery wagon comprised two launchers, seventy-two 4-pounder and sixteen 6-pounder rockets, eight short-range anti-personnel rockets, four incendiary and one illuminative, making a total of 101 rockets. The angled 'gutter' launcher, suitable for the Congreve stick rocket, had been superseded by a tripod launcher similar in appearance to a surveyor's theodolite].

The gun batteries were rifled muzzle-loaders (M1863) and were extraordinarily accurate. They fired shell, shrapnel, incendiary and cannister. Shell (fired in a low trajectory *geschlossen*) for the 3-pdr had a range up to 3,000 paces, up to 4,000 paces for the 4-pdr, and up to 5,000 paces for the 8-pdr. Shell (fired in a high-trajectory *geworfen*) had a range up to 1,800 paces for the 4-pdr and up to 2,000 paces for the 8-pdr. The incendiary rounds had a similar range to shell for both low and high-trajectory fire. Shrapnel was employed with the 3-pdr at ranges up to 1,500 paces, and up to 2,000 paces with the 4 and 8-pdrs. Each gun in a 4-pdr battery had 156 rounds with it, while those of the 8-pdr batteries had 128 rounds. In addition, the corps ammunition park had for each battery 622 x 4-pdr rounds and 512 x 8-pdr rounds. The army ammunition park had an extra reserve of 311 x 4-pdr rounds and 256 x 8-pdr rounds for each battery. Cannister rounds for the 4 and 8-pdrs were limited to ranges of 300–500 paces.

With each field artillery regiment was a park company, which was deployed to the corps and army ammunition parks in the event of war.

In the event of mobilisation, each regiment activated a depot company for replacement purposes and Nrs. 1, 2, 3, 4, 5, 7, 8, 9 and 10 activated a second park company.

Fortress Artillery

In 1866 there was no independent fortress artillery in battalion or regimental formations. Fortress artillery companies were designated within the complements of the field artillery regiments. In peacetime each field artillery regiment had four, in wartime five, such companies, which were stationed in the fortresses as well as in several of the larger cities.

In addition, there was a Coastal Artillery Regiment, which in peacetime consisted of four battalions with 18 companies and two 3-pdr mountain batteries, the latter 'en cadre'. In the event of mobilisation, four additional coastal artillery companies, four depot companies and two mountain batteries were activated. The wartime complement of a coastal artillery company consisted of six officers and 214 men. The Coastal Artillery Regiment had the following wartime complement: 168 officers, 6,136 men, 11 horses and 244 pack animals.

During the war of 1866, five companies of the Coastal Artillery Regiment were in Pola, one coastal artillery company and two depot companies were in Trieste, six coastal artillery companies were in Venice and the remaining ten coastal artillery companies and two depot companies, as well as the four mountain batteries, were in Dalmatia (Budua, Cattaro, Ragusa, Zara, Lissa, etc.).

The 60 fortress artillery companies were assigned as follows:

Krakau 4, Olmütz 7, Theresienstadt 5, Josefstadt 4, Königgrätz 1	21
Verona 11, Mantua 6, Peschiera 4, Venice 3, Legnano 2, Rovigno 1	27
In Borgoforte 1, Pola 1, Ulm 2, Komorn 1	5
With Brigade Kaim in the Tirol	3

With Brigade Hayduk in Istria	1
In Vienna	3
Total	60

Engineers (Genie-Truppe)

The Engineers consisted of two regiments, each of which was organised, in peace and in war, into four battalions of four companies each. In the event of mobilisation, a depot division [two companies] was activated for each regiment. On a wartime footing a regiment consisted of 98 officers, 3,690 men, 257 horses and 100 horse-drawn vehicles. During the 1866 campaign the companies of the two Engineer Regiments were assigned as follows:

Engineer Regiment Nr. 1:
1st Battalion was with the North Army at the disposal of the army commander.
2nd Battalion: three companies (6, 7, 8) in Olmütz and one (5) in Josefstadt.
3rd Battalion: three companies (9, 10, 11) in Krakau and one (12) in Königgrätz.
4th Battalion: three companies (13, 15, 16) in Vienna and one (14) in Theresienstadt.
The depot division was in Vienna.

Engineer Regiment Nr. 2:
1st Battalion was with the South Army. One company was with the army headquarters and each of the three army corps had a company.
2nd Battalion: 5th Company in Rovigo, 6th in Venice, 7th in Vienna, 8th in Dalmatia.
3rd Battalion: 9th Company was in Peschiera, 10th in Mantua, half of the 11th Company in Legnano and the other half in Istria with Brigade Hayduk, the 12th Company was in Pola-Triest.
4th Battalion: 13th Company with Brigade Kaim in the Tirol, 14th in Vienna, 15th and 16th in Verona.
The depot division was in Verona.

Pioneers

The Pioneers were organised into six independent battalions of four companies each. In the event of mobilisation, each battalion added a depot company. The wartime complement of a Pioneer battalion consisted of 23 officers, 1,209 men, 595 horses, 134 horse-drawn vehicles and four Birago bridge equipages, each equipped to bridge 42 *Klafter*3 or 79.6 metres.

---

3   Tr. Note – The Birago Bridge was a pontoon bridge introduced in 1841 and named after its inventor. Birago regularly describes widths of rivers to be spanned in *Klafter*, or 'fathoms' (an Austrian fathom measured 6 feet). (Karl Ritter von Birago. *Untersuchungen über die europäischen Militärbrücken und Versuch einer verbesserten, allen Forderungen entsprechended Militärbrücheneinrichtung* (Vienna: Anton Strauss's se. Witwe, 1839))

During the 1866 campaign, the Pioneer Battalion was assigned as follows:

1st Battalion was with the North Army at the disposal of the army command.
2nd Battalion one company with each of the 1st, 3rd, and 8th Army Corps of the North Army.
3rd Battalion was with the South Army Headquarters. The depot company was in Verona.
4th Battalion was with the South Army Headquarters. One company was in Venice.
5th Battalion one company with each of 4th (1st Company), 6th (2nd Company) and 10th (3rd Company) Corps of the North Army. The 4th Company was initially at the Vienna bridgehead, later with the South Army.
6th Battalion was with the North Army at the disposal of the army commander.

Trains

The trains were provided by the Military Transportation Corp [*Militär Fuhrwesens Corps*] which in peacetime consisted of 50 transport squadrons. Each such squadron had a peacetime complement of one officer, 52 men, 39 horses and 16 horse-drawn vehicles. In war these squadrons were responsible for bringing forward the ammunition magazine [*Colonnen Verpflegs Magazine*]. Each army corps and each Cavalry Division had such a magazine, to which in the first case four, in the second case two, transport squadrons were assigned. Each squadron had a wartime complement of two officers, 152 men, 224 horses and 51 horse-drawn vehicles. Furthermore, in the event of mobilisation 'Draught Horse Squadrons' [*Bespannungs Escadronen*] were activated as necessary to provide teams for the corps and army ammunition parks, the telegraph wagons, the corps ambulances, the military bridge equipages, the ambulances of the medical companies and so on. The complements of these squadrons varied, depending on the number of horse-drawn vehicles requiring teams. Every army corps and each army command had a Transport Replacement Depot [*Fuhrwesen Ergänzungs-Depot*]. Their complements varied, amounting to one tenth of the number of horses of all the horse-drawn units that were assigned to them for replacements. The number of men amounted to half the number of horses plus an additional 10 per cent.

Medical Service

The Medical Service consisted of ten medical companies, which in peacetime were stationed at Vienna, Laibach, Pest, Verona, Trient, Padua, Treviso and Graz. Each company had a peacetime complement of three officers, 97 men and 40 horse-drawn vehicles. In wartime, one medical company was attached to each army corps. These medical companies included (counting the horse-drawn squadron) five officers, one regimental surgeon, 270 men, 112 horses and 37 horse-drawn vehicles. For replacement purposes, at the start of mobilisation, two depot companies were activated. The Geneva Convention of 22 August 1863 for the improvement of the situation of soldiers wounded in war was first signed by Austria on 22 July.

Tactical Formation of the Army

An army corps consisted, as a rule, of four independent infantry brigades. Infantry Divisions [that is, a formation comprising two or more brigades] did not exist, having been disbanded after the 1859 campaign.[4] An infantry brigade usually consisted of two line or *Grenz* Infantry Regiments, with their first three battalions, one *Jäger* battalion and one 4-pdr foot battery. Attached to an army corps was one cavalry regiment, a pioneer company, an artillery and ammunition reserve, an ammunition column, one ambulance, one medical company, a Transport Replacement Depot and a Transport Field Inspectorate [*Fuhrwesens Feldinspection*].

In 1866, before the outbreak of the war, there were seven army corps as shown below. At the start of mobilisation, activation of three additional army corps, the 8th, 9th and 10th, was also ordered.

1st Corps	Bohemia
2nd Corps	Lower and Upper Austria, Salzburg, Steiermark
3rd Corps	Carinthia, Carniola, Istria and a part in Venetia
4th Corps	Moravia, Silesia, Galicia, Bukowina
5th & 7th Corps	Venetia and the Tyrol
6th Corps	Hungary, Siebenbürgen, Croatia

The cavalry brigades were formed from two to three cavalry regiments and one 4-pdr horse battery. Two to three brigades formed a Cavalry Division which was designated either 'heavy [reserve]' or 'light' according to its composition.

The artillery reserve assigned to each army corps consisted of three to five batteries and was designated the Corps Artillery Reserve. The ammunition reserve was designated Corps Ammunition Park. The North Army (but not the South Army) was still assigned an artillery reserve at the exclusive disposition of the army commander that consisted of 16 batteries organised into four divisions designated the Army Artillery Reserve. The activation of the army ammunition park belonging with this was effected by the Field Artillery Regiments.

Military Obligation

The military obligation to serve was set at eight years in the line and two years in the reserves, but men seldom remained for the full eight years in the present situation.

Supply in the Field

As a rule, the troops carried two to four days rations with them, two days rations on the wagons of the Brigade Supply Column [*Brigade Proviant Colonnen*], four days in the Corps Rations Magazine [*Corps Verpflegs Magazine*] and eight days in the [Army] Supply Rations Magazine

---

4   Author's footnote: The three corps (5th, 7th and 9th) of the South Army consisted of only three
     infantry brigades.

[*Nachschubs Verpflegs Magazine*]. Requisite replenishment of the stock of rations took place from the Main Field Rations Magazines [*Feld Verpflegs Hauptmagazines*] located further to the rear.

The Army of the Kingdom of Prussia

Since the War of Independence, the general military obligation in Prussia was nine years, three of which were under arms. From 1819 to 1851 the number of men in active service stood at about 122,000. In 1851 the peacetime strength was raised from 122,000 to 130,000 men. In 1857 the number rose to 141,000, and finally in 1858 to 200,000 men.

As a result of this reorganisation, in 1866 Prussia was able to put an Army of 325,000 front-line troops into the field with 864 guns, and mobilise an additional 68,000 reserve troops (fourth battalions) and *Landwehr* with 144 guns to follow the field army, while 114,000 replacement troops and 98,000 garrison troops remained behind. The overall strength of the [fully mobilised Prussian Army] thus amounted to 605,000 combatants.

The organisation of the Kingdom of Prussia's forces into eight army corps and 16 Divisional Regions [*Divisions Bezirke*] went into effect on 22nd December 1819 and has remained in effect ever since. The Guard Corps was not associated with any province but recruited from all the kingdom's provinces. In peacetime each of the eight provincial army corps was organised into two infantry Divisions, and each Division into two infantry brigades. One or two *Landwehr* infantry regiments were attached to each infantry brigade. In addition, two cavalry brigades belonged to each of the above army corps. One of these was composed of three and the other of two line regiments. Every cavalry brigade had two *Landwehr* cavalry regiments attached. Corps troops included one field artillery regiment, one *Jäger* battalion, one pioneer battalion, and one trains battalion. The Guard Corps was basically organised in the same way as a provincial army corps but differed somewhat in the number of troops.

In 1866 each corps (with limited exceptions) entered the field with eight Infantry Regiments. The ninth regiment of each corps was employed in the activation of new formations.

The main army operating against Austria consisted of 8½ corps of regulars and one corps formed from *Landwehr* which was designated the 1st Reserve Army Corps, and in addition, the detachments of Major General Knobelsdorf and of Major General *Graf* Stolberg (together totaling nine battalions, 12 squadrons and two batteries), which consisted in part of regulars and in part of *Landwehr* troops [Fontane devotes an entire chapter to these detachments and their deployment in Silesia.[5]] The Divisions of the 3rd and 4th Corps had no corps troops and were independent.

The West, or Army of the Main, consisted of 1½ corps of Prussian line troops, while the 2nd Reserve Army Corps consisted of half Prussian and half troops from several states of the German Federation that were fighting on Prussia's side.

A light field hospital and a section of a stretcher bearer company was attached to each Division. Each army corps had three heavy field hospitals, one stretcher bearer company, a horse depot, a field bakery column and five supply columns [*Proviant Colonnen*].

5   Theodor Fontane, *The German War of 1866: The Bohemian and Moravian Campaign*. Trans. Frederick P. Steinhardt. Ed. Gerard W. Henry (Solihull: Helion, 2021).

Infantry

Until 1859, each of the eight provincial army corps was organised into five line and four *Landwehr* infantry regiments, with the latter only existing '*en cadre*'. The Guard Corps consisted of two Foot Guards Regiments, two Grenadier Guards Regiments and one Guards Reserve Regiment, as well as four Guards *Landwehr* Regiments.

In addition to the Guards, the Army consisted of 40 line infantry regiments and 32 *Landwehr* infantry regiments, the line infantry regiments being numbered 1–40, seven of which, Nrs. 34–40, consisted of only two battalions and were designated 'Reserve Regiments'. Including these, the total infantry present (including Guards) amounted to 126 battalions.

In 1860 the existing 32 *Landwehr* Infantry Regiments were converted into the same number of line infantry regiments, with each new regiment receiving a number that was higher by 40 than the line infantry regiments that were in the same brigade as the *Landwehr* regiment. On this occasion the reserve regiments, each of which received a newly activated third battalion, were designated 'Fusilier Regiments'. In the Guard Corps, the 3rd and 4th Foot Guards Regiments, the 3rd and 4th Grenadier Guards Regiments, and the Guards Fusilier Regiment were activated.

In 1866 the infantry comprised 81 regiments, consisting of nine Guards regiments, twelve Grenadier Regiments numbered 1–12, fifty-two line regiments numbered 13–32 and 41–72, and eight Fusilier regiments numbered 33–40. The Guards Infantry consisted of four Foot Guards regiments numbered 1–4, four Guards Grenadier regiments numbered 1–4 and one Guards Fusilier regiment.

All the infantry regiments of the army had three battalions each. The Fusilier regiments had three Fusilier battalions; the Guards regiments, as well as the Grenadier regiments, each had two Grenadier and one Fusilier battalions; the line regiments had two Musketeer battalions and a Fusilier battalion as the third battalion. In the event of mobilisation, each regiment activated a replacement battalion. The wartime complement of an infantry regiment with three battalions amounted to 69 officers, nine officials, 3,098 men, 120 horses and 16 horse-drawn vehicles (3,086 combatants, including officers).

Each battalion was organised into four companies, each company into three platoons, one of which was designated a 'Rifle Platoon' [*Schützenzug*]. The rifle platoons of a regiment were numbered I–XII across the regiment, while the other platoons were numbered 1–8 in each battalion. For example, each Fusilier battalion (third battalion) consisted of Rifle Platoons IX–XII and Platoons 1–8.

The infantry was armed with the *Zündnadelgewehr* [needle-gun], which was manufactured by the Prussian firm Dreyse zu Sömmerda and first introduced into the Prussian Army in 1841, with an order for 60,000 pieces priced at 15 *Thaler* each. The rifles of the Fusiliers and *Jägers* were somewhat shorter than the other infantry rifles and were equipped with a sword bayonet while the rifles of the Grenadiers and Musketeers were equipped with *Stichbajonette* [a 'stab' bayonets with a narrower triangular blade].

The Fusiliers formed the army's light infantry. They were identified externally by black leather straps and belts, whereas the other infantry had white [*Beriemung*].

Of the 81 infantry regiments, 64 (8 Guards, 11 Grenadier, 39 line and 6 Fusilier regiments) were assigned to the army facing Austria. Another 14 [the author then breaks this number down into 2 Grenadier, 11 line and 2 Fusilier regiments, which comes to 15; however, the order of battle in the Prussian Staff History says 14] were assigned to the Army of the Main that was fighting in western Germany.

One regiment, the 62nd, was with Major General Knobeldorf's detachment operating in Austrian Silesia. The 4th Foot Guards Regiment started the war as the Berlin garrison, while the 63rd line regiment formed a part of the garrison of the Neisse Fortress.

In accordance with a directive of 18 June 1866, 48 fourth battalions were activated from the replacement battalions of all infantry and Fusilier regiments of the Guards Corps, as well as of the 1st, 2nd, 6th and 8th Provincial Corps, and of the 36th, 37th and 39th Fusilier Regiments. The strength of a fourth battalion was 802 men. On 3 July 1866 the fourth battalions were assigned as follows:

To the Army of the Main, those of the 30th and 70th IR and those of the 36th and 39th Fusilier Regiments	4
To First Army, those of the 33rd and 34th Fusilier Regiments	2
To Second Army, those of the 1st, 3rd, 4th, 5th, 41st, 43rd, 44th, 45th, 10th, 22nd, 23rd, 50th, 51st, 62nd, 63rd IR	15
To the Second Reserve Corps (activated with the fourth battalions of 2nd, 9th, 14th, 42nd, 61st and of the 1st, 2nd, 3rd and 4th Foot Guards regiments	10
To reinforce garrison troops in Berlin, those of the 1st and 2nd Guards Grenadier Regiments as well as of the Guards Fusilier Regiment	3
In Breslau, those of the 3rd Guards Grenadier Regiment	1
In Stettin and Colberg, those of the 21st, 49th and 54th IR	3
In Posen, those of the 37th and 38th Fusilier Regiments	2
In Schleswig-Holstein those of the 11th and 25th IR	2
In Hessen and Hannover, the 28th, 29th, 41st, 61st, 68th and 69th IR	6
Total	48

Consequently, Prussia had 291 battalions of line infantry available. Those replacement battalions from which the fourth battalions were formed achieved the prescribed strengths by taking in recruits. All 81 replacement battalions were employed either for garrison or occupation duties.

Jäger Troops

The Jäger consisted of eight battalions, Nrs. 1–8 and a Guards Jäger Battalion. There was one Jäger battalion with each of the nine corps (the Guards Corps had an additional Schützen Battalion [rifle battalion] which also counted as Jäger).

In the event of mobilisation, each Jäger battalion (and the Guards Schützen Battalion) activated one replacement company. The wartime complement of a Jäger (or Schützen) battalion was the same as that of a battalion of line infantry: 22 officers, three officials, 1,030 men, 40 horses and 10 horse-drawn vehicles (1,024 combatants, including officers). The Jäger and Schützen were armed with needle-guns and wore black leather straps and so on [Lederzeug]. In the course of mobilisation, a new 9th Jäger Battalion was activated from the replacement companies of the Guards Corps and also of the 1st, 2nd, 3rd, 4th, 7th and 8th Jäger

Battalions, while the above replacement companies were again brought up to strength with recruits. The 9th Battalion was assigned to the Army of the Main (Major General von Flies Division). The replacement companies of the 5th and 6th *Jäger* Battalions were employed to activate one *Jäger* company, which was assigned to the detachment of Major General *Graf* Stollberg. Thereby 11¼ battalions of *Jäger* were deployed with the field army, 10¼ of these against Austria.

Cavalry

Prior to 1859 the cavalry consisted of 38 regiments, 6 Guards and 32 line. These comprised 10 Cuirassier [unlike the Austrians, Prussian Cuirassiers did wear armour], 5 Dragoon, 10 Uhlan and 13 Hussar regiments. Each cavalry regiment was formed of four squadrons, so the cavalry of the standing army was 152 squadrons strong.

In 1859 the cavalry was increased by 48 squadrons, so Prussia had 200 squadrons that were organised in 1866 into 48 regiments: 10 Cuirassier regiments, including the *Garde du Corps* and the Guard Cuirassiers; 10 Dragoon regiments, two of which belonged to the Guards; 13 Hussar regiments, one of which belonged to the Guards; and 15 Uhlan regiments, three of which belonged to the Guards. The Cuirassiers and Uhlans, 25 regiments in all, formed the heavy [reserve] cavalry. The Dragoons and Hussars, 23 regiments in all, formed the light cavalry. Four Hussar and four Dragoon regiments had five squadrons, the others had four squadrons, giving a total of 200 field squadrons. One field squadron had a complement of five officers and 150 men. The wartime complement of all of the field squadrons totaled 30,000 horses. In the event of mobilisation each cavalry regiment activated one replacement squadron. The wartime complement of a cavalry regiment of four squadrons amounted to 23 officers, four officials, 650 men, 704 horses and seven horse-drawn vehicles (625 combatants, including officers). The replacement squadrons numbered 10,750 men.

Of the existing 48 cavalry regiments, in 1866 five (the 4th Cuirassiers, the 5th and 6th Dragoons, as well as the 8th and 9th Hussars) were with the Army of the Main. The 2nd Uhlan Regiment was with Major General Knobelsdorf's detachment [in Silesia]. The remaining 42 regiments were in combat against the Austrian North Army.

Artillery

By 1859 the artillery consisted of nine regiments, each regiment with three battalions, each battalion consisting of one horse, three foot and eight fortress companies [12 in total]. Each of the companies that was designated for field artillery service had four guns, giving a total of 48 [per battalion], 36 foot artillery and 12 horse artillery. In wartime the number of guns in each regiment doubled, thus an artillery battalion comprised 12 batteries of eight guns each [96 in total]. The wartime strength of the field artillery thus amounted to 108 batteries with 864 guns [three battalions x 96 guns in each x three regiments]. In 1860 the number of batteries was increased to 135, but in the event of war, these batteries were reduced to only six guns each instead of eight. In 1866 the artillery was organised into nine brigades: one Guard and eight line artillery. Each of these was divided into two regiments: one field artillery regiment and one fortress artillery regiment. A field artillery regiment now consisted of four battalions, one horse and three foot battalions. Each battalion consisted of four batteries of six guns each.

Accordingly, each field artillery regiment had four batteries (24 guns) of horse artillery and 12 batteries (72) guns of foot artillery.

The horse artillery had 4-pdr rifled breech-loading guns [also 12-pdr smooth bore muzzle-loading guns, see below]. Two batteries of each foot artillery battalion were equipped with either 6-pdr [rifled breech-loaders] or with 4-pdr [also rifled breech-loaders], respectively. However, at the start of the 1866 campaign, the re-arming of the artillery had not been entirely completed and about one-third [six-sixteenths] of all field batteries were still outfitted with 12-pdr smoothbores.

The 1st and 3rd foot battalions of a field regiment provided the two Infantry Divisions of each corps with artillery, while the 2nd battalion formed the corps artillery reserve. Of the 36 batteries of horse artillery in 1866, 11 were attached to the cavalry brigades, two to the 13th Infantry Division of the Army of the Main, and 15 allocated to the corps artillery reserve of the individual army corps, while eight batteries formed the reserve artillery of the 2nd Army.

Each field artillery regiment activated nine ammunition columns of 23–24 horse-drawn vehicles each, and one replacement battalion of four batteries, each with four guns that were employed as reserve batteries for the fortresses. The wartime complement consisted of, for a foot battalion of four batteries: 14 officers, four officials, 595 men, 488 horses, 41 horse-drawn vehicles and 24 guns.

For a single horse battery: three officers, one official, 150 men, 208 horses, ten horse-drawn vehicles and six guns. For the nine ammunition columns, aside from [civilian] staff: 20 officers, five officials, 1,503 men, 1,434 horses and 202 horse-drawn vehicles.[6]

The fortress artillery regiments each consisted of two battalions, and these in turn, of four companies, so that there were 72 companies of fortress artillery.

On 19 May 1866, the order went out for activation of a reserve field artillery regiment, which would be attached to the 1st Reserve Army Corps that was in the process of activation. This regiment consisted of three battalions of four 12-pdr batteries (72 guns) and two 6-pdr batteries (12 guns); nine of the 12-pdr batteries were with the 1st Reserve Army Corps and the other three (as well as the two 6-pdr batteries) were attached to the combined Division Beyer of the Army of the Main. The new 2nd Reserve Field Artillery Regiment, which was activated at the same time as the above, consisted of five 4-pdr and three 6-pdr batteries (48 guns) and was attached to the 2nd Reserve Army Corps, which was activated on 3 July 1866.

Technical Troops

The technical troops consisted of one Guard Pioneer and eight line Pioneer battalions. In the event of mobilisation, each of the nine Pioneer battalions activated a replacement company and an entrenching [Schanzzeug] column. In addition, the Pioneer force was responsible for activating six pontoon columns, six light field bridge trains, four telegraph battalions as well as 26 Pioneer detachments, the latter with a total strength of 3,193 men that were assigned for technical service in 26 fortified locations. In 1866 two additional reserve Pioneer battalions were activated for the 1st Reserve Army Corps. The wartime complement consisted of, for a

6   Author's footnote: During the 1866 campaign the artillery of the 1st Army (including the Elbe Army) fired 48 rounds per gun, and that of the 2nd Army, 28 rounds per gun.

pontoon column and for a light bridge train: four officers, one official, 197 men, 353 horses and 54 horse-drawn vehicles. For a Pioneer battalion (including entrenching column): 18 officers, three officials, 670 men, 106 horses and 20 horse-drawn vehicles.

Trains

The trains included one Guard train and eight line train battalions, which in the event of war, each had a complement of 36 officers, 117 officials and 1,841 men with 1,490 horses. Of these, 12 officers, 565 men and 213 horses were allotted for replacement purposes.
   A train battalion consisted of:

	Officers	Officials	Men	Horses	Carts
Five provision columns	10	10	480	805	160
One field bakery	1	2	110	25	5
One horse depot	1	1	47	89	1
Three heavy corps hospitals	3	59	244	193	35
Three Division hospitals	3	42	180	144	30
One stretcher bearer company	4	3	211	14	1
Staff	2	0	4	7	1
Sub-total	24	117	1,276	1,277	233
Additional replacements	12	–	565	213	–
Grand total	36	117	1,841	1,490	233

Landwehr

The Prussian *Landwehr* was called into existence on 17 March 1813. It received further legal basis in the *Landwehr* Order of 21 November 1815, and through the Cabinet Order of 22 December 1819, whose basic provisions were still in effect in 1866. The *Landwehr* was divided into two levées. The first included men up to the age of 32, the second up to age 39. According to the reorganisation plan of 1860, the first levée was to be used only to garrison fortified places, and the second strictly for defence of the Prussian provinces, and then only to be called up if an enemy had already crossed the border. In peacetime, cadres of 116 infantry battalions and 12 cavalry regiments existed, with a total of 1,971 men and 276 officers belonging to the first levée. In wartime, the *Landwehr* of the second levée also consisted of 116 infantry battalions of 800 men (total 93,000 men) and one squadron of cavalry of 100 horses could be activated for each battalion.

Landwehr infantry

The 116 battalions of the first levée formed 36 infantry regiments of three battalions each, two Guards, two Grenadier and 32 provincial *Landwehr* regiments, numbered 1–32, and eight independent battalions numbered 33–40. In peacetime four *Landwehr* infantry regiments were assigned to each army corps. As for the independent battalions, two belonged to 1st Corps, one each to 2nd and 4th Corps, and four to 7th Corps.

In 1866 employment of the *Landwehr* was not strictly in accord with the legal specifications. A portion of them were employed as mobile field forces outside the fatherland. In May, the 1st Reserve Corps, which consisted of two *Landwehr* Infantry Divisions and one *Landwehr* Cavalry Division, was activated. All four *Landwehr* regiments (12 battalions) of the Guard corps, as well as the 9th and 21st Pomeranian *Landwehr* Regiments (six battalions) of the 2nd Corps and the 13th and 15th *Landwehr* Regiments (six battalions) of the 7th Corps were employed to form the above two *Landwehr* Infantry Divisions. The two remaining *Landwehr* Regiments of the 7th Corps, the 16th and 17th *Landwehr* Infantry Regiments, formed a part of the Prussian occupation forces in Schleswig-Holstein. Each of these 30 battalions had a strength of 802 men.

The remaining 86 battalions, 62 of which had a complement of 802 men and 24 of which had 500 men, were employed as fortress garrisons, and then as garrison troops in the large cities of the homeland. In the Silesian fortresses the *Landwehr* infantry battalions of the 5th and 6th Corps provided garrison troops; six of these battalions belonged to the detachment of Major General *Graf* Stolberg. In the further course of the campaign, the *Landwehr* troops were withdrawn from the fortresses that were not endangered and employed as rear echelon troops in the occupied areas.

The *Landwehr* infantry of the 1st Reserve Corps was armed with needle-guns, while the other *Landwehr* battalions were provided with Minié muzzle-loading rifles. Only later in the campaign did the detachment of Major General *Graf* Stolberg receive needle-guns.

Landwehr Cavalry

The *Landwehr* cavalry consisted of 35 *Landwehr* regiments: two Guard, four Dragoon, eight Uhlan, twelve Hussar and eight heavy *Landwehr Reiter* regiments. Those of the Guards were assigned to the Guard Corps and from the others, four were attached to each of the eight provincial corps. Two *Landwehr* cavalry regiments were attached to each of the line cavalry brigades of the provincial corps.

In peacetime only 12 regiments had cadres, two of which were assigned to each of the 1st, 2nd, 3rd, 4th, 5th and 6th Corps. Accordingly the *Landwehr* regiments of the Guard corps, as well as of the 7th and 8th Provincial corps had no cadres, and only two regiments of the *Landwehr* cavalry regiments of the other corps had cadres. The other two remained without cadres. In 1866 six cavalry brigades were formed from the 12 regiments that had cadres. Three of these formed the *Landwehr* Cavalry Division of the 1st Reserve Corps, one was attached to the 2nd Army and one to the detachment of Major General Stollberg. Of the remaining cavalry brigade, one regiment was attached to the Army of the Main, and the other to the occupation force in Schleswig-Holstein.

Those *Landwehr* cavalry detachments that were planned for the fortresses were also activated in the requisite number. On 18 June 1866, 20 reserve *Landwehr* squadrons were formed from the cavalry detachments of the fortresses of the 1st, 2nd, 3rd, 4th, 7th and 8th Corps districts and formed into five regiments and two squadrons of Dragoons. Three of these regiments were attached to the Army of the Main, two to the 2nd Reserve Army Corps, and the Dragoon squadrons to the occupation forces in Hesse and Hanover.

Bibliography

Anon, *Exerzir-Reglement für die Infanterie der Königlich Preußischen Armee vom 25. Februar 1847. Neuabbdruck under Berücksichtigung der bis zum 3. August 1870 ergangenen Abänderungen* (Berlin, 1870)

Barry, Quintin, *The Road to Königgrätz: Helmuth von Moltke and the Austro-Prussian War 1866* (Solihull: Helion, 2010)

Bassett-Powell, Bruce, *Armies of Bismarck's Wars, Prussia, 1860–67* (Philadelphia, PA: Casemate, 2013)

Birago, Karl Ritter von, *Untersuchungen über die europäischen Militärbrücken und Versuch einer verbesserten, allen Forderungen entsprechended Militärbrücheneinrichtung* (Vienna: Anton Strauss's se. Witwe, 1839)

Craig, Gordon A, *The Battle of Königgrätz: Prussia's Victory over Austria, 1866* (Philadelphia, PA: University of Pennsylvania Press, 1964)

Dicey, Edward, *The Battlefields of 1866* (London: Tinsley Brothers, 1866)

Dolleczek, Anton, *Geschichte der Österreichichischen Artillerie, von den frühesten Zeiten bis zur Gegenwart* (Vienna, 1887; reprinted Graz: Akademische Druck-u. Verlagsanstalt, 1973)

Dolleczek, Anton, *Monographie der k. u. k. österr.-ung. Blanken und Handfeuer – Waffen* (Vienna: Kreisel & Gröger, 1896; reprinted Graz: Akademische Druck-u. Verlagsanstalt, 1970)

Fiedler, Siegfried, *Kriegswesen und Kriegführung im Zeitalter der Einigungskriege* (Coblenz: Bernard & Graefe Verlag, 1991)

Fontane, Theodor, *Der deutsche Krieg von 1866* (Berlin: Verlag der königlichen Geneimen Ober-Hofbuchdruckerei R.V. Decker, 1870)

Fontane, Theodor, Trans. Frederick P. Steinhardt. Ed. Gerard W. Henry, *The German War of 1866: The Bohemian and Moravian Campaign* (Solihull: Helion, 2021)

Friedjung, Heinrich, *Der Kampf um die Vorherrschaft in Deutschland, 1859 bis 1866* (two volumes) (Stuttgart: J.G. Cottasche Buchhandlung Nachfolger, 1916) [Original edition has valuable maps that are not in print-on-demand reprints. Friedjung also includes maps of actions in Italy.]

Gaertner, Richard, *Die ersten 15 Jahre des 3, Magdeburgischen Infanterie-regiments Nr. 66* (London: Wentworth Press, 2019)

Hozier, H.M, *The Seven Weeks War: Its Antecedents and Its Incidents* (two volumes) (Philadelphia, PA: J.B. Lippincott & Co., 1867) [The original edition has outstanding maps, which are second only to those of von Lettow-Vorbeck. Cost is moderate, and it is readily available.]

Jähn, Max, *Die Schlacht von Königgrätz zum sehnjährige Gedenktage des Sieges auf Grund der gesammten einschliglichen Literatur* (Leipzig: Verlag von Fr. Wilh. Grunow, 1876) [Contains 500 pages providing the most detailed account available of the Battle of Königgrätz.]

k.k. Generalstabs Bureau für Kriegsgeschichte, *Österreichs Kämpfe im Jahre 1866 dritte Band* [volume 3 of 4] (Vienna: Verlag des k.k. Generalstabs, 1868) [Useful for its extremely detailed account of the action and for superb maps. Be sure and check for presence of maps.]

Koch, H.W, *A History of Prussia* (New York: Dorset Press, 1978)

Kriegsgeschichtliche Abteilung des Grossen Generalstabes, *Der Feldzug von 1866 in Deutschland* (two volumes) (Berlin, 1867) [Official history by the Prussian general staff historical department.]

Lettow-Vorbeck, Oscar von, *Geschichte des Krieges von 1866* (three volumes) (Berlin, 1892–1899) [The original edition is worth locating, as it has the finest maps of all the significant actions of the war except Italy.]

Moltke, Helmuth von, *Moltkes Militärische Werke II, Die Thätigkeit als Chef des Generalstabes der Armee im Frieden, Moltkes Taktisch-Strategisch Aufsätze aus den Jahren 1857 bis 1871: Memoire an Seine Majestät den König vom 25 Juli 1868 über die bei der Bearbeitung des Feldzuges 1866 hervorgetretenen Erfahrungen,* and *Betrachtunge vom Frühjahre 1867 über Konzentrationen im Kriege von 1866* (Berlin: Ernst Siegfried Mittler und Sohn, 1900)

Moltke, Helmuth von,   *Moltkes Militärische Werke, III, Kriegsgeschichtliche Arbeiten, zweiter Theil. Kritische Aufsätze zur Geschichte der Feldzüge von 1809, 1859, 1864, 1866 and 1870/71, Betrachtungen über das Gefedcht von Trautenau am 27. Juni, 1866 und über die Kämpfe des V. Armeekorps bei Nachod, Skalitz und Schweinschädel vom 27 bis 29 Juni 1866* (Berlin: Ernst Siegfried Mittler und Sohn, 1899)

Müller, Hermann von, *Die Entwicklung der Feld-Artillerie in Bezug auf Material, Organisation und Taktik, von 1815 bis 1870: Mit Besonderer Berüucksichtigung der Preussischen Artillerie auf Grund Officiellen Materials* (Berlin: Verlag von Robert Oppenheim, 1873)

Ortenburg, Georg, *Waffe und Waffengebrauch im Zeitalter der Einigungskriege* [*Heerwesen der Neuzeit, Abteilung IV, Das Zeitalter der Einigungskreige, Band 1*] (Koblenz: Bernard & Graefe Verlag, 1990)

Ortenburg, Georg, *Waffe und Waffenbegrauch im Zeitalter der Revolutionskrieg* [*Heerwesen der Neuzeit, Abteilung III, Das Zeitalter der Einigungskreige, Band 1*] (Koblenz: Bernard & Graefe Verlag, 1988)

Rothenberg, Gunther Erich, *The Army of Francis Joseph* (West Lafayette, IN: Purdue University Press, 1976)

Rothenberg, Gunther Erich, *The Austrian Military Border in Croatia, 1522–1747* (Urbana, IL: University of Illinois Press, Urbana, 1860)

Schmidt-Brentano, Antonio, *Die Armee in Österreich, Militär, Staat und Gesellschaft, 1848–1867* (Boppard am Rhein: Harald Boldt Verlag, 1975)

Schwarz, Herbert, *Gefechtsformen der Infanterie in Europa durch 800 Jahre* (Munich: Selbstverlag, 1977)

Showalter, Dennis, *Railroads and Rifles: Soldiers, Technology and the Unification of Germany* (Hamden, CT: Archon Books, 1975)

Showalter, Dennis, *The Wars of German Unification* (London: Arnold, 2004)

Strobl, Adolf. *Königgrätz. Kurze Darstellung der Schlacht am 3. Juli 1866 mit 6 ordres de bataille und 38 Skizzen* (Vienna: Verlag von L.W. Seidel & Sohn, 1903)

Wandruszka, Adam & Urbanitsch, Peter, *Die Habsburgmonarchie 1848–1918, Banc V Die Bewaffnete, Macht* (Vienna: Verlag der Österreichischen Akademie der Wissenschaften, 1987)

Wawro, Geoffrey, *The Austro-Prussian War: Austria's War with Prussia and Italy in 1866* (Cambridge: Cambridge University Press, 1996)

White, Jonathan R., *The Prussian Army, 1640–1871* (Lanham, MD: University Press of America, 1996)

Winter, Frank H., *The First Golden Age of Rocketry: Congreve and Hale Rockets of the Nineteenth Century* (Washington, DC: Smithsonian Press, 1990)

Wirtgen, Rolf, *Das Zündnadelgewehr, Eine militärtechnische Revolution im 19. Jahrhundert* (Bonn: E.S. Mittler & Sohn, 1991)

Witte, Hans Joachim & Offermann, Peter, *Die Boeselagerschen Reiter, das Kavallerie-Regiment Mitte und. die aus ihm hervorgegangene 3. Kavallerie-Brigade/Division* (Munich: Schild Verlag, 1998)

The period 1815-1914 is sometimes called the long century of peace. It was in reality very far from that. It was a century of civil wars, popular uprisings, and struggles for Independence. An era of colonial expansion, wars of Empire, and colonial campaigning, much of which was unconventional in nature. It was also an age of major conventional wars, in Europe that would see the Crimea campaign and the wars of German unification. Such conflicts, along with the American Civil War, foreshadowed the total war of the 20th century.

It was also a period of great technological advancement, which in time impacted the military and warfare in general. Steam power, electricity, the telegraph, the radio, the railway, all became tools of war. The century was one of dramatic change. Tactics altered, sometimes slowly, to meet the challenges of the new technology. The dramatic change in the technology of war in this period is reflected in the new title of this series: From Musket to Maxim.

The new title better reflects the fact that the series covers all nations and all con ict of the period between 1815-1914. Already the series has commissioned books that deal with matters outside the British experience. This is something that the series will endeavour to do more of in the future. At the same time there still remains an important place for the study of the British military during this period. It is one of fascination, with campaigns that capture the imagination, in which Britain although the world's predominant power, continues to field a relatively small army.

The aim of the series is to throw the spotlight on the conflicts of that century, which can often get overlooked, sandwiched as they are between two major conflicts, the French/Revolutionary/Napoleonic Wars and the First World War. The series will produced a variety of books and styles. Some will look simply at campaigns or battles. Others will concentrate on particular aspects of a war or campaign. There will also be books that look at wider concepts of warfare during this era. It is the intention that this series will present a platform for historians to present their work on an important but often overlooked century of warfare.

For more information go to:
https://www.helion.co.uk/series/from-musket-to-maxim-1815-1914.php

Submissions
The publishers would be pleased to receive submissions for this series. Please contact series editor Dr Christopher Brice via email (christopherbrice@helion.co.uk), or in writing to Helion & Company Limited, Unit 8, Amherst Business Centre, Budbrooke Road, Warwick, Warwickshire, CV345WE.

Books in the series: